D0853427

The Maverick Way

Also by Richard Cheverton

"A Fine Madness"

"The Last Story"

THE MAVERICK WAY

Profiting from the power of the Corporate Misfit

By Richard Cheverton

With Bill Wilson & Lanny Vincent

Illustrations by Louis Dunn

maverickway.com

La Palma CA; San Rafael CA; Tucson AZ; Ogdensburg WI

For information, address:
MAVERICKWAY.COM,
7211 Monterey Lane,
La Palma, CA 90623

Or, check out the Maverick Way web site on the internet:
www.maverickway.com

First edition.

Library of Congress Catalog Card Number: 00-190537.

ISBN 0-9668226-1-7

Editing, proofing: Ann Haley
Cover painting: Craig Pursley
Book design & composition: Waypoint Books

Printed in the United States of America.

For Trena.

For Marg.

For Camille.

For Nancy.

It's not easy being married
to a maverick.

"When all right-thinking human beings are
struggling to remember that other men and women
are free to be different, and free to become more different
still, how can one honestly write a rulebook?"

Robert Bringhurst,
"The Elements of Typographic Style"

"You want proof? I can't give it to you. But let me tell you a story."

RobertTownsend,
"Up the Organization"

Contents

Innovation demands
systematic abandonment
of the established,
the customary,
the familiar,
the comfortable… .

Peter S. Drucker

Introduction.

THE FORBES BOO-BOO.

In its issue of March 3, 1997, *Forbes* magazine acknowledged it had made a mistake: "Twenty-one years ago, when the Kimberly-Clark Corporation decided to go head-to-head against Procter & Gamble in the diaper business, we predicted disaster. Kimberly-Clark was a maker of pulp and paper. What made it think it could take on the master of marketing? What a dumb idea.

"As it turns out, it wasn't a dumb idea. In fact, it was a smart idea. The architect of the Kimberly diapers strategy, Darwin Smith, retired in late 1991 and died in 1995 at the age of 69; but he lived to see his strategy vindicated."

How Kimberly-Clark did it is a tale of brilliant marketing and smart corporate thinking. With brand names such as Kleenex, Kotex, Huggies, Depends and Scott, Kimberly-Clark is now one of the largest consumer products companies in the world, with a return on equity and net profit margins that, *Forbes* said, "socks it to P&G."

This book is an in-depth examination of what went on behind the scenes to make this marketing so brilliant and the corporate thinking so smart—who made the essential innovations happen and how they did it.

Many factors contributed to the eventual success of Kimberly-Clark's transformation. Shrewd marketing, bright corporate thinking, strong management, sound fiscal control, constancy of purpose, yes. But, almost unseen, there were also significant innovations, courageous leadership, plus some very interesting people, relationships and innovation management maneuvers.

This part of the story has remained untold—even within Kimberly-Clark. It involves pivotal (but underground) individuals we characterize as "mavericks," "MOMs" (mentors of mavericks) and their protectors. Their behind-the-scenes actions create an implicit, informal and underground set of people, practices and relationships that stimulate innovations which provide the basis for corporate renewal.

We call this collection of people, practices and relationships "The Maverick Way."

The Maverick Way does not lend itself to precise formulas or step-by-step recipes. Instead, it is... well, *maverick.* It manifests itself in ways that are specific and peculiar to each corporation, shaped by the context and conditions specific to that corporation at that particular time. This makes it difficult, if not impossible, to directly apply the experience of one company to that of another. However, we obviously think there are lessons, if not encouragement, for other companies that face the problem of having grown too big and too detached from their original entrepreneurial vocations.

This book concentrates on the corporate world—particularly large corporations with established revenue streams. We limited ourselves even further in looking closely at the story of Kimberly-Clark during its remarkable transformation over a 20-year period.

We did so partly because such an in-depth look is rare; and partly because it seemed to us that by taking such a close-up view, we might uncover innovation management principles and practices useful to the reader.

MEETING THE MAVERICKS.

Many people were involved in making Darwin Smith's vision for Kimberly-Clark a reality. One such person, Bill Wilson, proved to be particularly prolific in the innovations he fostered. Bill, as both maverick and mentor to mavericks, acted as a catalytic wellspring for the innovations in product, technology, business and marketing strategy upon which Kimberly-Clark's metamorphosis was based.

While Darwin Smith articulated the ultimate goals and kept a steady hand on the helm, Bill worked the magic that brought reality to Smith's vision.

Bill would be the first to acknowledge that he did not act alone. In fact, he was at the center of a complicated web of relationships—all quite underground—that we call the maverick's "secret society."

In the pages that follow, you'll meet members of the secret society that played such a key role in this remarkable period:

- Fred Hrubecky, an engineering maverick who made diapers that worked and could be mass produced.
- John Raley, currently Kimberly-Clark's manager of intellectual property, who arguably has become Bill's successor.
- Leo Shapiro, Bill's life-long friend, a social and corporate prophet, and a "listener" to products.
- Dick Loescher, another of Bill's confidants, who acted as a maverick "spotter," and gate-keeper.

You'll meet key figures who nurtured the Maverick Way and discover how they protected mavericks:

- Leroy Peterson and Peter Larson (currently CEO of Brunswick Corporation), the executive vice presidents who "rediscovered" Bill and gave him tacit permission to collect "legitimate crazies." It was Larson who challenged Bill to "teach the organization to do what you do."
- Richard Sonnentag, another executive vice president, who unwittingly found himself "supervising" Bill just before Bill's retirement, and who arguably became more savvy than others to Bill's magic.

In the 1980s, I reported to Bill and was involved in his attempts to fulfill Larson's challenge to "teach others" what he did so successfully. After I left Kimberly-Clark in 1985 there was an embarassingly long hiatus in our relationship, but when I finally reconnected with Bill we both knew that the unfinished "project" was still staring at us. I remember saying to Bill that I was up for finishing this project, but only if he was, too. With a deep and somewhat resigned sigh, but not without a little twinkle in his eye, Bill replied with his trademark "yes."

Our first step was to recruit—or was it seduce?—Richard Cheverton to help us complete this project, not only because of his skills with words but because he understood what we were talking about. Chev had experienced the "belly of the beast" of corporate renewal and innovation management firsthand, albeit in another time and place—*The Orange County Register*'s celebrated attempt to redesign the way the news is produced.

Chev started to realize that working with Bill was having a transforming effect on his own life. Like most of us who have worked closely with Bill at one time or another, Chev was beginning to experience the contagious and transforming power of Bill's peculiar combination of hope, courage, maverick magic, freedom and even love.

After many false starts, Chev conceived the form of this book as a series of conversational reflections between a maverick and mentor and his protégés. So what started out as a dialogue between a veteran maverick and his younger (though aging) pupil ended up being transformed into a "trialogue," and initiated a now-growing network of mavericks and their protectors who offer each other support and counsel and comfort as only other mavericks can. Chev also urged me to sponsor a couple of roundtables—an intimate gathering of a few mavericks and maverick "protectors" who are continuing to meet together each year to compare notes and exchange views and experiences. (See **www.maverickway.com** or **www.innovationsthatwork.com**).

LESSONS LEARNED.

Originally, I thought we were going to create a book that was about the special role that mavericks and their protectors play in corporate renewal. It is that. But it is also about personal change and transformation. It speaks to the very human themes of freedom, courage, exploration and love—placing them in the context of where a majority of our waking hours are spent: at work.

A goal of this project has been to contribute something new and valuable to the field of innovation management. As always, we have built upon the thinking and writing of others, both published and unpublished.

However, we believe we have taken a different point of view than most, by focusing on mavericks and their relationships, and especially the role of the mentor of mavericks (MOMs) in the conception, development and politics of corporate innovation. What we learned as a result of "going deep"—and the winks of recognition from many different people for what is captured in these pages—suggest that the Maverick Way may also be practiced in educational, governmental, non-profit and even ecclesiastical contexts. It has convinced us that the Maverick Way is both as old as humankind's aspirations for freedom, purpose and achievement—and as new as your current innovation efforts.

Chev, Bill and I hope that you not only enjoy reading what follows, but that you might also refer to it from time to time for inspiration and wisdom, and find in it the transformative power of freedom and love in your corporate context. It's the Maverick Way.

LANNY VINCENT
March 10, 2000
San Rafael, California

Dreams are excursions
to the limbo of things,
a semi-deliverance from
the human prison.

H.F. Amiel

1.
A Curious Dream.

The Call.

The phone call came, as such things do, without warning. It was from an old acquaintance. His name was Lanny Vincent, and he was a management consultant. I did not hold that fact against him.

I had not seen Lanny for some time. I knew that he had been busy building his new practice after leaving in some sort of messy ownership shuffle at Synectics Inc., the Cambridge, Mass., consulting firm. We had one of those not-quite-pals business relationships—hearty hellos shouted across a busy airport concourse, occasional "just checking in" e-mails, that sort of thing.

Now he had a pitch: to write, or more accurately, rewrite a book that had been penned some twenty years ago, a book that had been written about the innovation process at one of his old employers, the Kimberly-Clark Corporation, those wonderful folks who bring you Kleenex and Kotex and Huggies and a raft of other products.

It was a book, Lanny said, that had been written and then promptly chucked down the corporate memory-hole.

"Why?" I interrupted.

"Because it turned into a book about one man, my old boss, Bill Wilson. And Kimberly's cultural antibodies are very anti-heroic and since the book focused on Bill that view was politically incorrect."

"If this Wilson character is as plain-bread as his name, he sounds pretty harmless," I said.

Lanny laughed sardonically. Bill was a "management Rasputin." Whenever something new and innovative happened at the staid, old Midwestern tissue-maker, "Wilson was usually around. Maybe not in charge of the project or even assigned to it—but just... lurking."

Wilson, Lanny added, had been a successful executive at K-C (as nearly everyone associated with the company abbreviated it), had started whole new product lines, created company divisions, run the corporation's European operation, done early work on environment and energy.

But, more importantly, he had been a mentor to dozens of K-C executives, Lanny included. "He ran a kind of secret society," said my friend cryptically.

"How did you get sucked into this?" I asked.

"I reconnected with Bill because I wanted to talk to him about my career. I felt like I was in a maze, not sure what route I would take out. So I wanted to reconnect with him for that selfish reason. And I found something much more. It was..."

And then Lanny used a word I hadn't heard before in a business environment: "...love."

The word hung there for a long moment.

"Why the book?" Lanny asked rhetorically. "It might be something that Bill said to me when I left Kimberly—

something along the lines of still expecting something from me. I ignored that; I figured Bill didn't have any influence on me. For ten years our relationship was dormant. When I reconnected with Bill, I realized that the book hadn't been finished. It's down in Bill's basement—hundreds of notes on file cards. And now it's time to finish it."

I started a mini-lecture on why a book is a crap-shoot; asked the standard skeptical questions about who would spend money to read about this unknown fellow.

None of which daunted Lanny in the least. "I don't give a darn if anyone reads this," he said with his trademark giggle. "I have to do this. *We* have to do this."

I started to resume the cold-water shower, but Lanny interrupted. "Why don't you come up to Tiburon and meet Bill? He'll be here this weekend."

And I heard myself utter the word, "yes."

It wasn't a decision: it was a feeling, an intuition, a sixth sense that somewhere in the background I could hear dice rattling. Besides, Lanny was paying for the ticket.

THE MEMORY.

I hung up the phone and stared into midspace for a moment. I wasn't sure I was completely comfortable with allowing Lanny Vincent back into my life. After all, Lanny and his colleagues from Synectics had done what consultants do best—destroy the status quo at a place that seemed to be humming along rather nicely. A place where I happened to be working.

It was a California newspaper, *The Orange County Register*, where I was an editor in charge of the paper's features coverage, lord of everything from recipes to book reviews. I loved my job, in the slightly fanatical, manic-depressive way that most journalists approach the business (which, of course, isn't a "business," but something quasi-religious, a morally superior attitude that makes journalists so tedious at parties).

Back in 1990, unbeknownst to the 300 innocents in the newsroom, the paper's top editor, N. Christian Anderson, had been seized with a desire to develop a grand new vision for the newsroom. And to help us to achieve the vision, Anderson hired some gunslingers from the consulting firm with the formidable name.

Lanny was one of them. He was the preppy one in sweaters and chinos and Bass loafers, as opposed to the one in the custom Armani suits, whose tailoring made the off-the-rack types in the newsroom so very, very nervous.

I sensed that Lanny, unlike some of his colleagues, had a good heart; that he actually believed in what he was doing. He was happy, bouncy, always up; he had an infectious, delighted giggle that was amazingly disarming. He was obviously smart—not just a guy with sheer mental wattage, but possessed of an awesome ability to listen and then distill the erratic, this-way-and-that of a meeting into its pure essence, to hear what you intended to say. Which is to say that peppy, preppy Lanny Vincent was also intimidating as hell.

A year later, Anderson and the Synectics crew had turned the newsroom every which way but loose. Considering that journalists devote their careers to covering change, usually violent, stupid or accidental, it came as a shock when change arrived in our very own workplace.

There were a few indignant resignations. Those of us who stuck it out ran the gauntlet of reinventing news beats, redefining job descriptions—there was even talk of reapplying for our jobs. The indignity of it all!

When the smoke cleared we were known in the cosseted world of big-city journalism as "The Newsroom Without Walls." Whereas the old *Register* had been made up of mutually distrustful duchies (mine among them), now everyone could and *should* write for every section of the paper—business writers filing stories for the sports section, for example. If it seemed like much ado about almost nothing... well, you'd be right. Funny, though: it didn't seem so harmless at the time.

Meanwhile, all of this reinvention had landed me in a new job. It had a grandiloquent title—managing editor for strategy and administration—but no one to actually manage, let alone any real power (at least in the sense of being able to issue an order and have someone hop to).

As near as I could tell, this new job was akin to being a Soviet commissar for the permanent revolution, a sort of in-house, full-time consultant. All very new-age, cutting-edge, cool.

But then Anderson ascended the corporation's greasy pole, becoming associate publisher. His successor had her *own* notions about the newsroom's vision. Another newsroom nabob became her right-hand man; his lip would curl dismissively around the dreaded word "Synectics."

And here I was—the Synectics Guy. Traveling nowhere on the slow boat to irrelevance. But there was no going back: There was someone else, someone new and full of bright ideas sitting in my old office back in the beloved features section. And that's when Lanny called.

THE MEETING.

Lanny picked me up at the San Francisco airport and drove me through rainy streets to a trendy Marin County restaurant: lots of heavy German automotive metal in the parking lot, tinnitus-inducing decibels inside.

Bill was waiting for us. He looked a lot younger than his seven decades: a full crop of silver hair in a Reaganesque pompadour; granite jaw; arctic blue eyes that, I mused, could probably do a pretty good job of intimidating, given the right circumstances. He wore a butter-yellow crewneck sweater—I wondered if it was an unconscious reference to his Wisconsin address, way back there in the land o' cheese curds and apple cheeks. He shook hands warmly, but at the same time seemed a little shy, maybe a bit wary.

As the grub arrived, Bill fussed with his bread, gave the avant-garde waiters and waitresses a skeptical look. The conversation was typical "opening the kimono" stuff: Bill had been born in 1923 in a place called Hamilton, Ontario (which explained his accent). That would make him 75 years-old. He looked darned fit for a septuagenarian.

He had retired from K-C back in 1988 after putting in a total of 42 years with the company. His final stop on the career ladder had been something called vice president of innovation management. (I felt a weird twang when he pronounced that job-title—clearly, we might have some notes to compare.)

Now he was living half the year on his 193-acre Ogdensburg, Wisconsin, farm; half in a cozy townhouse in Tucson, Arizona. He was married, four kids. He regretted not spending more time with them while they were growing up: "I was a workaholic."

These days, he stayed busy—"I collect a few things here and there"—and dabbled in some new companies, including one that had domesticated milkweed fiber and turned it into stuffing for quilts. In short, he seemed the ideal picture of the active, AARP-type senior: alert, fit, busy and with enough socked away in the bank to list two addresses on his personal stationery.

But—a book? The worm of skepticism was turning…

THE STORY.

Bill had brought along the original book—a misnomer, since it was a Xeroxed typescript ring-bound under a transparent plastic cover, more an overstuffed report than anything else, by the looks of it. The title seemed pretty weighty: "The Case of the K-C Innovator, a Handbook on Introducing Change." It was written by one Rose Moss. (A *nom de plume?* I wondered. But, no, it was the real thing.)

I flipped through the manuscript. My eye caught the following chunk: "In our first conversation I was looking for clues to (Bill's) success, and I noticed something very distinctive. Whenever Bill mentioned something he had done he mentioned people he had worked with. It seemed to me that his mind was like a map, full of names that identified places in time, in his own history, and those names were the names of people."

Sure enough, every time Lanny threw out a name or date, Bill would respond with a long—sometimes *very* long—story. Here's a typical one:

"I was vice president of Exploratory Projects (*Bill*

was named to that job in 1982). A group of fellows—they didn't work for me and I didn't really know them—came to me with a hell of an idea. I said, 'Gee, this is terrific. Why aren't you doing it?'

"They said, 'We don't have permission.'

"I said, 'Go talk to so-and-so.'

"'We did and he turned us down.'

"I suggested a few other people, but they had struck out there, too.

"I said, 'Hey, you guys, what the hell do you want from me?'

"They said, 'We want permission.'

"'Fine. I give you permission.'

"They laughed. 'You can't do that, Bill. You can't give us permission.'

"'Why the hell not?'

"'We've gotta have a number. A cost-center.'

"'OK, you got a pencil? Seven-nine-eight-six-three-four-two.'

"'Whose number is that?'

"'What the hell do you guys care? You asked for permission and I gave you permission. You asked for a number and I gave you a number—what the hell else do you want?'

"Of course, they hadn't spent more than two or three thousand dollars until the vice presidents who had turned them down started fighting for their project.

"Three years later, I was asked to give a talk about innovation and I used this as an example. I said, 'If you have a good idea, just go do it. Never mind asking for permission, never mind going through a bunch of rigmarole. If it isn't any good, hide it. Nobody wants to know anyway. If it's terrific and looks like it's great, they'll give you all the money you want. Just go and do it.'

"At the break, the woman who runs the research budget came up to me and said, 'You know, I got that number. I couldn't figure it out. It looked legitimate. It had the right numbers in the right sequence. I tried to fit it in here and there and everywhere.'

"'So where did it wind up?'

"'In the president's discretionary fund. He never noticed a thing.'"

It was a cute story, worth a chuckle or two, but it also bothered me, as did some of Bill's other tales of corporate derring-do. What was this guy—some sort of organizational merry prankster? If I had tried to pull that kind of crap in the *Register* newsroom...well, the outcome was too terrible to contemplate.

Another thought concerned me: Bill seemed awfully *pleased* with what he had done. I didn't know if his story was an invitation to join his happy conspiracy—or a warning that the elderly gentleman might be capable of some dangerous tricks.

Maybe it was both, but I didn't have time to think that

through because Bill was off and telling another story… and another…

I interrupted the monologue. "What's this book about?"

And, to answer, Bill rattled off a string of homilies that seemed awfully like clichés. "You can get what you want if you're willing to pay the price," and "Don't take no for an answer," and "It's easier to ask forgiveness than permission." I doubted that Bill had been the first executive to utter those phrases—but, even if he had, that didn't seem to be a strong enough armature to begin sculpting a book.

The discovery.

I went to bed in Lanny's guest room that night convinced that I was about to bail out of the project. I had all sorts of reasons. Instead of a quick cut 'n' paste, this was looking like the literary equivalent of pulling teeth; a mass—more like a mess—of stuff that just didn't seem to fit together.

Bill didn't seem to be good timber for the kind of CEO-worship that was clogging the bookshelves. In this "winner-take-all" society, he had never made it to the tippy-top of the greasy pole. Nor was Kimberly-Clark a paragon of hip management like, say, GE or Microsoft. It had some great products: Kleenex was practically generic for tissue, Kotex literally brought an age-old problem of feminine hygiene out from under the counter—but, in most cases, they had been developed a half-century ago. Even worse, Bill was a man of big, throbbing, block-long machines churning out warehouses full of products, stuff that got sold across the counter in brick-and-mortar stores. Now, as any schoolchild knew, the electron was king. Heavy iron was being disintermediated by kids with bad haircuts and MBA's.

As I thought about that, I flipped through the Moss book and found this unsettling passage: "Wilson had received line management promotions. He had shown that he could run a business. But the way he ran a business was not like the way anyone else ran a business at Kimberly-Clark.

"He worked efficiently, but without the appearance of efficiency. He allowed a margin of sloppiness to show. He did things bordering on the illegitimate. He siphoned off profits from one business to promote another without permission. He defied explicit instructions from his principal. He scandalized many of his colleagues who were careful about appearances as well as about actually keeping control. What Wilson interpreted as flexibility, they interpreted as incompetence, or worse."

I snapped the book shut and contemplated another current running through my mind: a vague fear that I was about to open the door to a fellow who would invade my psyche, rearrange all the furniture, then depart without a word of explanation. I had seen how Bill had gotten under Lanny's skin. And how he had stayed there for more than a decade.

I had enough phantom memories and regrets, thank you very much. Better to back out early, cut my losses.

And so, feeling oddly comforted, I drifted off to sleep.

I had a sort of low-grade dream, the kind that plays itself out in the gray hours just before you wake up. I was sitting at a desk. It was barren—except for a book. I picked it up. It was small, hand-sized, more like an engineer's handbook: battered, well-handled; a hip-pocket kind of volume. It had slightly tarnished letters embossed on the cover that spelled out one word:

Maverick.

I popped awake in my strange bed in a strange room and contemplated the word that had arrived unbidden from dreamland.

Granted, it was as American as a knuckle-sandwich; a word that spoke, in its three syllables, of our peculiar love-hate relationship with the outlaw, with the lone holdout on a hanging jury, with the dead-end kid knocking off the nabob's hat.

But that was also the word's *problem*—it seemed synonymous with "pain in the ass." Square peg, round hole. The nail that sticks up and must be pounded down.

Maverick—as a manager. I knew that these misfits were awfully entertaining to have kicking around the newsroom, but only if they didn't work for you. They were always popping up in the strangest places, kiting the wildest ideas… nosy, not quite trustworthy, infuriating. I recalled the times I had been hauled into the editor's imperial presence to hear a complaint about some stunt that one of my errant troops had pulled, and my embarrassment in admitting that, gee, I hadn't known anything about it.

"You *should*," he would snap.

So, I wasn't quite sure what to do with this disquieting word. I couldn't even call it a concept; certainly not a book-length premise. But it seemed, in some strange way, to bundle what Bill had done into a nice three-syllable package. Maybe it was a small thought that I could leave behind as a going-away present…

THE QUOTE.

After breakfast, we adjourned to Lanny's office. Feeling a little embarrassed, I told them about the dream. When I mentioned the word "maverick," it triggered one of Lanny's memories.

He had been running a consulting gig at a large chemical company, leading a brainstorming group that had developed all sorts of interesting ideas, whereupon (being engineering types) they had locked-up on the nitty-gritty of actually implementing these wonderful new ideas.

"What you really need," Lanny said, "is a maverick." And he remembered the response: a flutter of nervous laughter, and someone muttering, "We fired them in the last restructuring."

"Hard to write a book about people who are constantly disappearing," I quipped.

"But not impossible," said Lanny, with one of his trademark giggles.

I muttered a few disconnected phrases: maverick was a "hard" word; not much of a sympathetic character—after all, the original Sam Maverick, a 19th century Texas land baron, had put his name into the language by leaving his cattle unbranded. Therefore, any newborn (and unbranded) calf wandering around on the free range belonged to him. It was a viewpoint that didn't endear him to his neighbors.

"Darned if I know what that has to do with *management*," I muttered as Bill peered at me intently, like a scientist studying an interesting bloom in a petri dish. Wordlessly, he reached into his wallet. He pried a battered, much-folded piece of paper from between the cards and currency.

He unfolded it and placed it on the table. This is what it said:

General Mathew B. Ridgway once asked five senior officers from the various services: 'What do you think is the most important job of the chief of staff?'

They did not know.

Ridgway answered: 'To protect the maverick, because only the maverick makes progress.'

Now my dream—the word that had popped out of nowhere—took on a spooky new significance. Damned if Bill Wilson hadn't had that little mantra in his billfold all along.

"Well, what the hell," I said. "My plane doesn't leave until this evening. Might as well keep talking…"

New wealth is created not by prophets but by heretics. They are the ones who not only challenge the way a business runs but offer an entirely new way of thinking about an industry. Not satisfied with something better, they want something different.

Gary Hamel

2.
MAVERICKS.

HITTING A MOVING TARGET.

The tools of Lanny's consulting trade are big, flapping pads of paper and miles of masking tape that wallpaper notes around a room. When he picks up a Sanford indelible pen, Lanny goes into brainstorming mode with an intensity that can be more than a little daunting.

Now Lanny gripped the pen. It poised, expectantly, over the empty white page.

OK, so we had a word—Maverick—but what the hell did it mean? How did the word and Bill's career intersect? Was Bill a one-off manager; so unique that his experiences had little to offer to others in the business world? How could we turn Bill's scattered experiences into the usual "Ten Steps to Nirvana" that seemed to be a requisite of a respectable biz book? And what if…

"Whoa!" said Lanny a little testily. "First things first: Let's try to define just what constitutes a maverick."

Bill stepped up to the plate. "A maverick does the unexpected and goes against conventional wisdom," he said eagerly. I started to frame a question, but Lanny gave me the evil eye: The essence of brainstorming, as I well knew, was to dump as many ideas as quickly as possible without stopping to critique or "discount" them. So, we dumped, as Lanny's pen made nervous *skritch-skritches* across the rapidly filling paper.

"A maverick attacks widely-accepted ideas and

beliefs that bind us to the commonplace." "A maverick is energized by statements such as: We can't do that because... We don't have the resources... It's not our area of responsibility..."

I had heard those excuses before. Sometimes coming out of my very own mouth.

"A maverick is an individual who thinks and acts in an unpredictable manner that results in new insights into innovative ways to live."

"A maverick appears to be a troublemaker, but is really acting with boldness and directness without regard to immediate consequences."

Then Bill obligingly supplied "Alternative words," a veritable flood: "Nonconformist, obstinate, troublemaker, mischief-maker, malcontent, rabble-rouser, individualist, free spirit, independent, eccentric, loner, free thinker..."

"In other words..." I interrupted.

Bill wasn't finished: "...against the rules, skeptic, self-sufficient, self-contained, self-motivated, inner-directed, footloose and fancy free, freewheeling, ungoverned, autonomous, self-regulating, unattached, unaffiliated, enjoying liberty..."

"...in other words, he's a royal pain in the ass," I laughed.

"Let me recite something George Bernard Shaw wrote," Bill said, intoning in his best Ontario drawl:

"'*Reasonable men adapt to their environment.*

"'Unreasonable men adapt their environment to themselves.

"'Thus all progress is the result of the efforts of unreasonable men.'"

"Which means?" I asked.

"The difference between a pain in the ass and a maverick is getting things done. Accomplishment."

"That's why Kimberly-Clark never fired Bill," Lanny giggled.

"So, the difference between the maverick and the pain in the ass," I said, "is that the maverick is dissatisfied with the way things are—and does something about it, instead of simply bitching about it?"

Lanny and Bill nodded emphatically. What makes the maverick so infuriating (to control-freak managers, such as myself) is also the key to their success.

They're bureaucracy-busters whose secretive back-channels unclog sclerotic lines of organizational mis-communication. They recruit ad hoc teams of like-minded, fast-moving conspirators (without getting anyone's permission, therefore short-circuiting the organization's tendency to say no). Their very sneakiness keeps vulnerable innovations off the corporate radar screen long enough for ideas to take some quiet test flights. And if they crash and burn? No big deal—or not as *big* a deal as if the project had been high-profile and, therefore, highly political.

"So the maverick gets things done?" I asked. "But what are those… *things*?"

"The maverick," Lanny intoned, "creates freedom…"

"…most people view it as 'freedom from,'" Bill interjected. "The maverick sees it as *freedom to*. Freedom is a different sort of power."

"And the maverick creates freshness," Lanny added.

"Freshness?" I interrupted. The word seemed a little *soft*.

"Call it renewal," said Lanny. "It could be in the context of a corporation developing new products, new businesses. It could be in the context of an organization in which management, processes and systems need revamping."

"All companies are looking to grow," said Bill. "There are three ways they do that: acquisitions—making a deal, when they don't know what else to do."

"Acquisitions have a terrible track-record," said Lanny. "Only the investment bankers win."

"Second," said Bill, "the company buys its own stock. When a company does that, I say to myself: They don't have any place to spend their money that's *new*. When a CEO is in that kind of situation, he'd better find a maverick."

"So the third choice for an organization is renewal," said Lanny.

"In other words, innovation," I said.

Lanny shook his head. For such a nice guy, he can be brutally direct when you've missed a point.

"'Everyone's an innovator' is complete BS," he said. "The conventional thinking is, more ideas! But the organization has antibodies that reject too many new ideas. It can't handle the ideas it produces now."

"But the maverick knows how to evade those antibodies," Bill grinned.

Still, it seemed to me, this creature was awfully elusive, a will-o'-the-wisp.

Lanny agreed.

"When you brand somebody, when you call someone a maverick," he said as his pen paused, "in a way, it's an oxymoron. You're branding the unbranded. There's an ambivalence about branding, categorizing, that the maverick resists because it constrains his or her freedom."

"But how does a manager *see* a maverick?" I demanded.

"The maverick should have a sly grin on his face," said Bill. He had a sly grin on his face.

"Like the wind, mavericks are seen by their effects," said Lanny after he had pondered a moment. "You can't identify a maverick directly. They're unbranded, right? You know them only indirectly, by the residual effects of the maverick having been 'here.' You can only follow the maverick's trail after he has made it."

"*Whew!*" I laughed. It *did* seem a little metaphysical.

"The maverick lives with the herd but isn't a *part* of the herd," said Bill, bringing us back to the metaphor.

"Look at it this way," Lanny said. "Bill had autonomy, but he also had anonymity. The maverick is part of a secret society."

"*Whew!*" again.

INSIDE THE MAVERICK'S SECRET SOCIETY.

This "secret society" stuff is exactly what makes managers, such as myself, perennially paranoid—the sense that the troops out there on the production floor or in the executive rat-warren or in the newsroom are *up to something*. And because it was hidden, probably on purpose, it couldn't be anything very good.

As we chatted I remembered the nights I had gone home after putting yet another edition of the *Register's* feature section to bed, fearful that I had gotten behind the curve, that I was missing something, that I was woefully under-informed about the little rustlings in the newsroom's underbrush—creatures of the night!—things that I *should* know and didn't. Things that would hurt. Bad.

I didn't question that paranoia. After all, that's what I was being paid for—*to run things*. Right?

And now Bill was revealing the dirty little secret: All through his four decades at Kimberly-Clark, he had been running his own herd. He was one of *them*.

"Did you round up a lot of 'unbranded' strays?" I asked as diplomatically as I could. "I would guess your herd was all over the company."

"Which is why he was disliked," Lanny interjected with a giggle. "Because a lot of those people reported to someone else. And that's what drives managers crazy."

"I would deal *between* divisions," Bill grinned. "In many cases, I was the guy in the middle. That's why I got so many dog businesses and misfit people dumped on me.

"I knew one fellow who was a maverick. His boss, who was in charge of the consumer division, wanted to get rid of him. I took the guy in. He was in all the supermarkets and variety stores, all the clients knew him, the district managers, and regional managers he'd been working with never really let him go when he transferred over to me. His old boss never knew about it.

"Eventually, it got to the point where I would market *my* new products through his old contacts in the consumer division. The division head didn't know."

"So, the maverick knows there are always people in the herd who will follow him," said Lanny.

"Even if they have someone else's brand on them," I said, trying to hide my anxiety.

"A maverick pays no attention to the brand," said Bill.

Which, of course, prompted a story:

In 1959, after working his way out of the mills to

Kimberly-Clark's headquarters in Neenah, Bill was named director of new products. Soon thereafter, "I took a group to Tomahawk, a resort in the north woods of Wisconsin, for a week. There must have been a dozen guys. Not all of them worked for me. We spent a week exploring all kinds of industries that we thought K-C might get into and that would be profitable ways to capitalize on our technology.

"These twelve people all agreed that if we were running K-C, we would get into the health-care business. But since we weren't, we had to do it on the QT. None of us ever spoke about that around K-C. I never told my boss."

"When you're talking about real innovation," said Lanny, putting on his best consultant's thinking cap, "by definition you're going to take an organization into a place where it's never conceived of going. So therefore there's no logical sponsor. Organizations today don't know how to act without a sponsor. So they spend a lot of time thinking about a sponsor, getting a sponsor in position—and then they go out and try to develop a business opportunity.

"But it doesn't take them into a new category or new market, because the organization has kept the sponsor inside the company's boundaries. So these guys formed a secret society—they created their own sponsorship."

"Over the next couple of years," Bill continued, "all

of the people who attended that meeting were feeding ideas back to me, still committed to the fact that we're gonna put K-C into this business whether they like it or not. One fellow left New Products, went back to the paper division, and for ten years he kept feeding ideas back to the group. When somebody fed a product concept back to us, we would make some and sell it into the hospitals. We didn't make a big thing of this to anybody. We called it, Make a little, sell a little.

"When we got an assignment from the head of the consumer division to 'Make Kleenex so strong that not even Paul Bunyan could blow through it,' one of our guys got the idea of cross-laying sheets of tissue on a layer of cotton fibers. We called it tissue-fiber laminate, TFL. We took that back to the consumer people. They said it was too expensive and they couldn't sell it.

"We said, OK, this is a great product to go into the health-care area. So we quietly started making sheets and pillowcases and gowns. Nobody asked us to do this. Nobody said, 'Wilson, put us into the hospital-products business.' There wasn't any place I could go to get sponsorship. There wasn't any executive vice president who had any responsibility for selling anything to hospitals."

"Didn't you have people saying, 'Bill, this is pretty dangerous. Shouldn't we check with someone?" I asked.

"Oh yeah, sure."

"So, what did you say to them?"

"If you know what the answer will be, why ask the question? If your chances are about fifty-fifty of getting a no, don't ask the question. Now's not the time. When we've developed the products and have a plan laid out and know how to do it—then we'll go talk to them. But up until that time, we're wasting our time and energy."

"I'd maintain that not many organizations would tolerate that kind of behavior," I said. "It would be a pretty major transgression."

"Well, it *was*," said Bill, looking awfully pleased.

"There are now three major divisions at Kimberly-Clark," said Lanny. "One of them is health-care."

COLLECTING.

"So, a maverick rounds up strays," said Lanny, writing the word in big letters on the pad. "Stray ideas, stray management tools. Stray ideas, trends, projects and seemingly unrelated people. Character transcends expertise. It's not just what people know, but how they think. For example, Bill always wanted the 'wrong' people in brainstorming sessions."

"If you put two physicists in a room you'll get consensus," said Bill. "Put a chemist and a physicist next to each other and you'll get conflict—which is what you want."

"Conflict?" I interrupted. "That's not politically correct."

Bill contemplated that for a moment. "Conflict—anger, that's what puts the steam in the boiler. We found out that if some of your anger is directed toward a person, it's very wasteful. What we want is anger directed at the problem. That's using anger to mobilize all of the brain's resources. Anger allows you to use your imagination more effectively."

"I remember that Bill would make me so doggoned mad," said Lanny, "because if we had a conflict in our group, he would immediately say, 'I can learn from this.' People would get angry all the time but Bill had an uncanny ability not to get caught by it. Because, if you're interested in collecting conflict, you don't get caught in it.

"So, the maverick is a collector, a commingler of reality," Lanny added, as always trying to stitch the thread into the larger tapestry. "He stirs the pot. The difference between a deal-maker and a maverick is that the deal-maker just puts two pots on the stove next to each other. The maverick mixes everything into *one* pot.

"It's Bill's greatest passion in life—collecting. Collecting and connecting. The maverick collects in order to connect and to see what happens out of that connection."

"I'll tell you a story," Bill said. "A manager once asked me for advice about finding engineers for a project. I suggested that he get a bunch of plywood, two-by-fours, hammers, saws, put it out in the middle of the space where they're going to work and when the first engineer comes in, tell him, 'Make yourself a desk or whatever you want and find a corner to put it in.'"

"Why did you give him that advice?" I asked.

"You find out whether or not you've got a guy who can do something. You tell some guys to do that and they'd say, 'Piss on you. You get me a desk like they got over in engineering or I'm leaving.' And the thing to say is, 'Good-bye.' If you want mavericks, it's a way of testing people."

THE INTELLECTUAL VACUUM CLEANER.

Bill's passion for collecting went into overdrive in 1957, when Kimberly-Clark's head of research asked him to create an entirely new unit ("I was assigned to come up with ways to make our professionals more effective, efficient, creative.") that came to be called the Operational Creativity Group, O-C for short in the hyphen-happy company.

The O-C Group became nothing less than a giant, intellectual vacuum cleaner, sucking up ideas, people, trends—a "skunk works" before the term was declassified.

Bill assembled a library on creativity. He dispatched his young staffers to collect "trends." He collected esoteric academic opinions—nothing was too far-out for consideration.

But, most of all, in the maverick way, he collected *people*. He collected a young Cambridge, Mass., psychologist named W.J.J. Gordon, who was doing research on how people behaved in business meetings (which is to say, badly). Bill Gordon would tape-record the meetings and, in surely one of the most onerous tasks in the annals of science, play them back, listening for clues about where meetings worked and, more often, ran off the tracks.

Later, when Gordon linked up with a collaborator, George Prince, Bill essentially turned Kimberly-Clark into a laboratory for the partners' fanciful ideas. From that work evolved Synectics. The firm Lanny had wound up at; whose gig at *The Orange County Register* led to my friendship with Lanny. As Bill unraveled his story, I got a queasy chill: circles within circles. Or, maybe, something more akin to a Mobius Strip.

But that wasn't all Bill collected. He seemed drawn to the misfits, the folks who could make a bureaucrat's blood boil. One, a White Russian expat named Serge Bouderline raised the ire of K-C's personnel department by demanding to know where the slums were in Appleton, so he could live there. Personnel refused to hire Bouderline.

"I had to put him on as a consultant because I couldn't get over that hump," said Bill with a wry smile.

"Why did you hire this guy?" I asked.

"He had changed his course, jumping from physics to government to business administration," said Bill.

"Some would see that as a minus," I said.

"Most people would. I always saw it as a fantastic plus. Because here's a guy who is saying, 'I don't want to spend my life in one spot.' He's willing to go over the cliff." He paused a beat. "Same as Lanny…"

I knew that Lanny had been trained as a minister and that, somehow, he had gone from the Presbyterian pulpit to Kimberly-Clark in the 1980s, when Bill's career had come full circle and he was running yet another internal think-tank known as Exploratory Projects. But that was all I knew and all that Lanny had ever seemed willing to tell me—that old consultant's distance-thing, I supposed.

Now Lanny talked of his crisis of faith, not in his religious beliefs (which continue strongly), but in his feelings about the church as an institution.

"A member of the church was a retired vice president of human resources for Kimberly-Clark. He listened to me and said, 'You need to talk to Dick Loescher (pronounced *Lesh*-her), he's kind of a maverick.' He used that term."

"Who was this guy Loescher?" I asked.

It turned out that Bill had collected him 24 years before, back in Bill's days heading the Operational Creativity Group. Although Loescher had gone on to become the company's head of purchasing, he was still a charter member of Bill's wide-ranging secret society.

"I set up an appointment with Dick," said Lanny. "He was sitting behind his desk, very rotund. He looked at my resume. He could probably see that I was a little dejected, a little frightened. Here I was with three years of Ivy League seminary and four or five years of promising ministerial experience. I felt like I was throwing it away.

"He said, 'Tell me about yourself. What do you really enjoy doing?'

"I said, 'Preaching.'

"'Tell me what's involved in preaching.'

"I said I worked through scripture, interpreting it, trying to put together a communication that would mean something to people.

"And then Loescher said, 'I know what you do. You're an interpreter. This company needs good interpreters. Hell, the world needs good interpreters. The only difference is that you're not going to work with one book but a lot of them.'

"In that instant he reached across his desk and metaphorically picked me up, dusted me off, set me right and shoved me out the door a new creature. It was an absolutely transformative moment. I believed that he knew what I did. He reframed it and gave me back my vocation.

"He ended the interview saying, 'I know this guy Wilson and he's putting together this internal think-tank thing. You're just the kind of guy he's looking for.'

"I had an interview with Bill and he hired me."

"You were making a significant change in your life," said Bill. "You were taking your ass in your hands and walking to the end of the plank."

I heard a note of almost fatherly pride in Bill's voice—and something else. The emotionally-loaded word that had occurred to me in my first conversation with Lanny.

I heard love.

It didn't seem to deflect Lanny and Bill the way it was distracting and discomfiting me. I thought about jumping in with a question, but then thought better of it. To be honest, I didn't feel like getting into *that* managerial minefield. As Tina Turner sings, "What's love gotta do with it?"

Instead, we turned back to the issue of spotting the maverick, retracing the slime-trail back to the creature itself. Gradually, as Lanny's pen skritch-skritched, we devised a set of questions for an enlightened manager to ponder:

"When you gave a person an assignment, did he come back not only with a solution, but with a broader and deeper understanding of the assignment? Did you learn something new, whether you wanted to or not?

"Does she sometimes 'forget' to tell you when the project is complete? Instead, does she get interested (or, as others say, 'distracted') by what she learned during the project and where it might lead? When you point this out, does she offer you a proposal for where to go next?

"Does he demonstrate manifest impatience with what's mainstream (i.e., if it isn't broken, he sets out to break it and fix it; or better yet, reinvent it)?

"Does she have a voracious curiosity—insatiable, in fact—that others complain is taking her 'out of her area'? Does this curiosity always seem to lead to some new invention and/or adventure?

"Does he tend to expose 'conventional thinking' as just that, by pointing to the facts and/or insights that he has discovered?

"Does she respond better to rewards that allow a broader freedom to do what she sees as appropriate, rather than rewards that deliver position or recognition—or even money?

"Does she sometimes seem insane—and do her craziest notions have a crazy way of becoming inventions?

"Is he always probing to uncover what the 'real' problem is—even when digging it out will rock the corporate or social boat?

"Is she more interested in inventing new tools than in polishing or perfecting old ones?

"Does he resist being governed by the tyranny of the need to show results?

"Does he have an irritating propensity to move at his own pace, even though he is always moving?

"Does she court hara-kiri by seeking out her most unremitting critics to help with her most sensitive projects?"

It was a pretty good questionnaire—and, oddly enough, I really didn't want to take it myself. Was it because I feared I would flunk? Or that I would pass?

I glanced up. The windows in Lanny's office had darkened, reflecting three very tuckered-out people who had, we realized, just begun to peer into a very deep pool, one filled with many interesting (and, quite possibly) dangerous creatures. And might be bottomless.

But that work would have to wait until we met again, which we arranged to do in a couple of weeks at Bill's snowbird base in Tucson. Meanwhile, we had our *real* lives waiting for us: Lanny off city-hopping, his frequent-flier miles relentlessly accruing. Me, back to the *Register* newsroom—a place, I sensed, I would be looking at rather differently in the future.

Never show fools
unfinished work.

R. Buckminster Fuller

3.
CONFESSIONS OF A HIGH-TECH MAVERICK.

Two ways of looking at Shark.

EXPLORING THE 'BLEEDING EDGE.'

I was still skeptical—aided by being back on my home turf, where skepticism is a handy survival tool. It still bothered me that Bill was, well...*old.* How, I wondered, did the younger maverick fit in the high-powered, fast-moving world of the technological bleeding edge, where, one could argue, every new corporation is, itself, a "maverick"?

I shared my concerns about that with Lanny.

"I'll call Scott," he said, explaining that his friend worked as an up-and-coming player at a very hot, very fast-growing Internet infrastructure company. A week later, I was back on the shuttle, off to meet a high-tech maverick.

(*"Scott" isn't his real name—we've changed it, and the name of the company where he works, which we'll dub "Rainbow," to preserve his ability to operate in the maverick's fragile "secret society." In light of what follows, we think you'll understand.*)

Scott and Lanny and I got together in a private dining room in a restaurant perched at the tippy-top of San Francisco's Bank of America building. Scott, as it turned out, had done a brief stint at Kimberly-Clark several years ago. His Kimberly-Clark days weren't entirely happy.

"I wasn't perceived as a team player," he recalled. "I

sought refuge with people of like minds, so that's how I fell into the relationship with Bill and Innovation Management. I remember meeting with him. I could tell he was kind of looking to see if I could find and develop a market on my own. But rather than give me a lot of help, he gave me hints. I think he was kinda testing to see how maverick I was, how far I'd take my ideas and run with them.

"I remember Bill telling me, 'Do what you want and don't worry about the consequences.' He said, 'If it's ten percent, stretch it. Just get your work done and stretch it out.'"

After Kimberly-Clark, Scott made a run at being an entrepreneur, developing a nifty product that made it to market but drained his bank-account in the process.

"I still have that entrepreneurial bug in me," Scott mused as we sat admiring the view. "I can't get it out. It's manifesting itself today at Rainbow. The nice thing is, I'm finding a way to make it work this time. The path was curved but I wound up in the right place."

"What are you doing now?" I asked.

"I'm a project manager," said Scott. "I'm technically in Purchasing, building the Internet connection with our suppliers and within Rainbow. It's a lot of systems work. The thing that's interesting is that it's like developing a product. You've got users, customers, suppliers, so to some extent I'm the CEO of my project. I see my boss once a week in a staff meeting and he lets me go, partly because I'm in an area where he doesn't have a lot of expertise."

Scott's project, as we spoke to him, was coming to a critical pass. It involved building a digital model of the firm's supply base, a massive undertaking that was bumping up against the limitations of computers—and the company's internal politics.

To get the job done required moving from desktop computers to the Internet. The company already possessed a division that worked with online data, but, as Scott explained dispassionately, "They don't do it well."

Scott's solution to that problem was simple. He developed his own, more effective tool. In the maverick way.

"I went outside and contacted the top companies in decision support systems," he said. "I did it on my own."

"Authorized?" I asked.

"Unauthorized. But I knew I had to do it. And no one stopped me because I just didn't tell 'em that I was doing it."

I asked what about his potential liability, the corporate moo-pies he could stumble into.

"Rainbow's Management Information Systems division would stop me."

Ahhh, I thought. The priesthood of dancing electrons, down in their air-conditioned chapel.

"And they did try to stop me a number of times," said

Scott. "I just ignored them. I said, 'Hey, I'm just doing research, I'm just looking. I'm not making any decisions, I'm not implementing anything. You stopping me from looking?'"

To throw off the MIS types, Scott kept renaming his project every time it popped-up on the radar screen.

"I refer to 'Decision Support Systems (DSS).' I describe it in as non-threatening way as I can—real generic. Now, MIS is catching on and saying, 'But that's technology,' so I'm going to have to change the name again. And soon that'll become a technology and I'll have to come up with another name. I gave a presentation yesterday and an MIS manager was in a room off-site, listening in along with Jim, who's my boss's peer. When I mentioned the latest name, the MIS manager said, 'We haven't decided we're going to call it that.' Jim said, 'It's generic, don't worry about it.'"

"He's protecting you," I said.

"Yes," said Scott. "My boss isn't good at that. He has a butt-heads relationship with the MIS manager, so I actually distance myself from him."

"You told me that you were about to go underground," said Lanny.

"I have," said Scott. "The first system we put up online—I knew that it wouldn't do what we wanted with the technology that we're using. I realized that this thing wasn't going to scale. But, even so, when I show the reports, management goes, 'Wow,' because they've never seen this kind of data. They say it's great and I say, 'This is nuthin'.'

"There's patience involved," Scott added. "And timing. I couldn't have gone underground six months ago with this and succeeded. I needed the existing system to be up so I could deliver something. Now I'm credible, plus now I've got something to compare against."

PROTECTING THE MAVERICK WITH A WINK & A NOD.

Now Scott is bringing in an outside consultant to help him create a state-of-the-art data system. MIS had tried hustled the consultant out the door, but Scott talked him into working with Rainbow on the come. If the project succeeds, Scott will scrounge up the money. Somehow.

"I tried to sell the project above-ground," said Scott. "I did try to sell it. And I didn't get anywhere with it. I made a couple proposals to my boss and to Jim and even to Roy (director of a group that uses Scott's tools) and they turned me down. And they've been turning me down for a year."

"Why?" I asked.

"They have other battles," interjected Lanny. "If Roy had some chips to spend, would he back it?"

"Jim will and my boss will, eventually, if it works," said Scott. "I'm not worried about it."

"Are they aware you're doing it without permission?"

"I've told them. I told Jim; I told a couple of people I'm going to do it. I told Jim's boss that I had this guy who would do it for free and he just gave me a knowing smile and walked away.

"A couple of days ago, I gave the consultant the data. He's running it. Meanwhile, I asked Jim to cover my back on this—I asked him to fund this if it's successful. *Only* if it's successful. He didn't respond.

"I met with my boss to talk about this technology and I proposed overtly again, 'What if we position this as a living specification, which is what MIS wanted.'

"I met with Jim today and we agreed that we'll try to get someone from MIS to sit in, so we're not doing this on a rogue basis. We'll fund it, just have somebody there from MIS so we can all learn together."

"You've got to find a maverick over there," I said.

"We won't," said Scott. "There isn't one. Doesn't matter."

"Really?"

"It doesn't matter at all. Because here's what we're gonna do. I've talked to Jim about it—I looked him in the eye and I said, 'I'm doing it. It's in progress. Monday, the consultant will have the calculations done; by the end of the week he'll have some basic reports done and two weeks after that he'll have the system done and in a month we'll be able to compare apples to apples—the technology that we have now versus the new technology.

"'Here's how I want to position this: nobody's going to know we're doing it. We're going to write a specification that matches exactly what we're doing. Then we're going to take that specification to MIS, market it to them, get them to agree to do it with us. We'll fund it and then we'll bring the consultant in and every week or so he'll deliver a piece that he's already done.'"

"And Jim said?"

"Jim said, 'Yes.'"

FINDING A PLACE TO HIDE.

Scott thought for a moment as a waiter slipped silently in and out of the room.

"Funny thing—I don't know if it's going to work. But at least I'll find out. Yesterday I was thinking, 'What the hell am I doing? I'm four months away from most of my stock options being vested. Nobody's asking me to push this. I could sit back and the VPs are happy with the reports they're getting now. What am I pushing for?' And I came to the conclusion that it's the challenge. The finding out. It's doing something new and different."

"What's in it for you?" I asked.

"I intend to use it to get a promotion."

"To what?" I asked. It seemed an un-maverick remark.

"I'm not worried about the title," Scott answered, "so much as the added credibility."

"And what does that give you?" Lanny asked.

"More freedom."

"What'll you do with the freedom?"

"Find the next cool thing," said Scott.

"All of this says to me that the principles and practices and paradigms that we're working through and trying to articulate about mavericks are the same whether you're at Kimberly-Clark or Rainbow," said Lanny as the waiter served final cappuccinos.

"The concept is the same," said Scott.

"But—you know where I'm going—where is there a difference?" Lanny asked.

"The difference is the pace," said Scott. "In some ways it's a cloak. Everybody's moving so fast that it's easier to go underground. Nobody has time to know that you're there."

It's so beautifully arranged
on a plate—you know
someone else's fingers
have been all over it.

Julia Child

4.
Tools in the Maverick's saddlebags.

GOING FORWARD BY LOOKING BACK.

A couple of weeks later, Lanny and I ventured to Bill's winter digs to continue our exploration. Bill picked us up at the Tucson airport and drove us to his condo tucked inside one of those ubiquitous Sunbelt gated communities. As we approached the automatic gate at the guardhouse, Bill floored the big van. At the last second before impact the robotic arm snapped smartly upward in a mechanical salute.

"Been trying to hit the damned thing since I moved here," Bill muttered.

As we toured the Wilson digs before getting down to business, I was struck by the stuff occupying every nook and cranny: platoons of tin soldiers marched across cabinets, shelves groaned under the weight of gold nuggets, slabs of copper ore, big crystals of quartz, snowball-sized chunks of turquoise. (Bill picked Tucson as his winter retreat because the biggest gem and mineral show in the world takes place there every February.) He gestured dismissively at the hoard; it was but a hint of what he had in his farmhouse back in Wisconsin. That's where he had the real collections, everything from toys and games to... *tractors.*

Collecting. It was one of the maverick traits that we had briefly explored in Tiburon. Now here it was, embodied.

We settled around the kitchen table, as Bill's wife,

Marg, served bologna sandwiches tidily swaddled in Saran wrap. She regarded us with a kind of motherly indulgence, as though we were kids about to cook up some kind of essentially harmless mischief.

I asked where the two of them had met—nice, safe chit-chat over the kitchen table. Bill said he had first spotted her at the University of Toronto, where she was one of two women in the engineering class of 1942. It must have been lonely, scary even, for a woman cracking into that boy's club. Marg not only broke in but, as Bill explained proudly, she was an honor student, close to the top of her class.

So… Bill had married a maverick?

"Yup," Bill chuckled.

I confessed that I wasn't really sure where to start unraveling the mystery of Bill Wilson, discover what made him tick as a maverick.

"Try the beginning," said Marg dryly, as she cleared away the dishes.

So, Bill gave us a quick autobiographical tour. As it unfolded, he began to supply tantalizing insights into the question: What creates a maverick?

Bill Wilson grew up amid the big trees and black flies of Haileybury, a small town in the wilds of northern Ontario. He was the product of local gentry: His mother, Mary, was a strong-willed woman, a nurse, a community leader. His father, Gordon, a physician, ran a big TB sanitarium—in those days, the disease was a widespread, relentless killer.

His father died young: Bill vividly recalls his father reviewing his own chest x-rays, scanning them, then diagnosing himself with congestive heart failure.

"He was always outspoken," said Bill. And, just maybe, a maverick. Bill recalled that while his father, a young Canadian Army officer during World War I, was bound for the European killing fields, he received two sets of orders. "One was to go to an artillery unit. The other was to go back to Canada and finish his medical training. As he was crossing the English Channel, the wind blew one of those orders into the ocean."

As a kid, Bill did things his own way, rewriting the rules as he went. When a friend got into money trouble, Bill "bought" his paper route, then put his pal on salary. Then he leveraged the route into a side-deal with the local laundry to pick up and return dry-cleaning. He had a downtown shoe-shine stand (his mother wasn't so fond of that, but Bill wouldn't give it up—to hell with appearances).

As Bill grew older, this son of local nabobs went off to work in a gold mine, then worked in a munitions factory on "the angel walk"— "One misstep with the nitroglycerine and you're singin' with the angels."

"Tell 'em about old Walter Paul," Marg prompted. Bill laughed at the memory.

"He was an old trapper, an old reprobate. The young girls around town had better look out."

He met the old trapper by chance: Bill and a buddy had bought a wrecked canoe and had meticulously repaired it. But they couldn't figure out how to form the vessel's "belly."

"So we asked Walter. He says, 'That's simple: You just fill it with hot water and the water just forces it into shape.'

"We did it, and there was our canoe, easy." But it wasn't entirely Bill's boat: "Walter would constantly borrow it and put oarlocks on it and row it like a rowboat."

Lanny laughed. "I was brought up with rowboats and canoes. There's something sacred about a canoe. A canoe is an environmentalist symbol of purity and ideals—you don't put oarlocks on a canoe. It's sacrilegious. It wasn't even Walter Paul's canoe, but he put oarlocks on it anyway, screw boundaries, private ownership."

A pretty good working description of a maverick, I thought.

Bill and Walter became the town's most improbable pair. They would disappear into the bush for days, living off the land. It was part Huck Finn, part Outward Bound.

"Walter never used a compass, never owned one. He'd teach me to always turn around, look where I'd been, where I'd come from. That was such a built-in thing that when I went to college down in Toronto, and I'd take

Marg out, we'd be walking down Yonge Street and I'd turn around and look back and see what the buildings looked like."

"Would it be extreme to say that's a metaphor for the way you navigated through life?" I asked.

"I suppose I always knew how to travel out of something I'd gotten myself into," said Bill, a smile playing across his face. "Sometimes you go straight through something and sometimes you retreat. When we were in a brainstorming session, we'd start to focus and drive down a certain path and I'd say, Let's stop. Let's go back to the beginning. Let's obsolete what we've done."

"Why would you do that?" I asked.

"Over the years I've learned that the first idea you come up with is probably not the best one. It's the second or third or fourth one down the line. The first one tends to be rather complicated and the best ideas are very simple.

"You've got to be careful of identifying the solution with yourself. It's part of the maverick's strength. The maverick says, I'll steal anybody's idea, doesn't have to be mine."

LYING-CHEATING-STEALING.

Lying? Cheating? Stealing? A maverick's strength? Bill had tossed off the comment casually but, still, there was something both exhilarating and disturbing about it.

"Sounds like one of a maverick's tools in his saddlebag," Lanny chuckled, as his pen *skritch-skritched.*

But what would such a motley collection of so-called tools contribute to the maverick's success?

Bill searched for the answer by (what else?) telling another story.

"I was in New Products (*circa 1960*) and we had just developed a scrim-reinforced nonwoven. It was a bunch of nylon threads coated with glue. When the glue was still wet, we laid a very thin coating of short cotton fibers on there, which gave it a very soft feel. It was developed as a cover for Kotex pads. Two nonwoven machines replaced a thousand looms in Berkeley, North Carolina and five-thousand looms in Westfield, Massachusetts.

"We had a small machine in research and the engineers unrolled a sheet of Kleenex on either side of the nylon threads. And that's what we called K-2000, eventually Kaycel. We didn't know what to use it for. The women in research took this material and made costumes for a party. One secretary made a little ballerina costume."

Word got around about the material—remember the famous "paper clothing" fad in the late '50s? It came out of Wilson's lab. "The 'I've Got a Secret' TV program wanted a starlet to be dressed in all-paper clothing. So we hired the fashion designer Vera to design a dress for Janet Blair and she wore it on the program.

"Finally, one of our sales guys, a real bird-dog, found a doctor in Detroit who wanted to start making disposable 'packs' for the operating room out of this material."

"Packs?" I asked.

"It's everything necessary for an operation: the sheets that provide the sterile field, a cover for the instrument stand, bandages—everything is in this pack." The new Kimberly material was ideal because it could stand up to the heat and pressure of sterilization procedures. It quickly began replacing cumbersome, infection-prone linens.

"By this time Jack Kimberly (*then Kimberly-Clark chairman, the last Kimberly to hold an executive position in the company*) and Bob Stevens (*the textile tycoon*), who were great friends, decided that maybe there was going to be something in this whole area of nonwovens. Stevens had a little nonwovens plant up in Massachusetts and we had this stuff, Kaycel, so they formed a joint venture, Kimberly-Stevens.

"This new company's major customer was something called Ruby Products, an outfit in Milwaukee that was making these new packs.

"Ruby said to Kimberly-Stevens, 'I can't afford Kaycel any more; I'm losing money on these packs. You've got to cut your price.'

"Even though I was only in charge of New Products, Kaycel's technical aspects were under me, so I was intimately involved. When Ruby demanded that we cut our price, I said, 'No way.'

"One of the Kimberly-Stevens executives came over to me and asked me to go down to Ruby Products and find out if he's really losing money on packs." But the Ruby operation was so complex, "I said the only way we could figure it out was to take the pack business out of Ruby and set it up independently so we can control it and find out what the costs are. The Kimberly-Stevens executive listened and said, 'OK.'

"As we were getting ready to set up this business, I went down to see Darwin Smith, who was head of the legal department—he later became Kimberly's chief executive officer.

"I said, 'Darwin, I'd like you to form a company for me, please.'

"He said, 'I can't do it.'

"I said, 'If you won't do it for me I'll go outside and hire somebody.'

"'If you go outside and do that you'll get fired.'

"I said, 'Darwin, I'm going to form a company. Now will you help me or not?'

"So, Darwin rapped the table and said, 'This is a meeting of Embezzlers Incorporated.'

"We called it "Convertors, Inc.' Darwin couldn't spell and neither can I, so that's why it's spelled with an 'or' instead of 'er.'"

Wilson recruited associates in New Products to create the company outside of Kimberly-Clark's base in Neenah, to avoid hassles with both management and the company's powerful unions—cheating, in other words. Then he set up the new business in an abandoned plant in depressed Oshkosh.

"Two of my people, Fred Hrubecky and Marion McCurry, were in charge of the operation. We hired a bunch of local women to do assembly. And then we sent the packs to American Hospital Supply and other customers.

"One day my boss, Bill Wright, came down to see what we were doing. He said, 'My God, we don't have the authority to do this. Shut 'er down.' So we shut it down.

"These thirty women in Oshkosh came in to see Fred and Marion and they said, 'Look, you kids, we know you're just starting this business and trying to get going and you obviously have some money problems—we kinda like this job and we'll work for nothing.'

'Fred said, 'We've got your phone numbers and we'll call you if we need you.'

"After we closed it down, the executive who was head of the hospital section in American Hospital Supply Corporation—he later became chairman of the board—jumped on the company plane and flew up to see Wright. He said he had dozens of hospitals depending on us and had orders to fill and we couldn't shut it down.

"So we called the women and started it up again.

"A while later I got a call from Wright and he said Jack Kimberly and Bob Stevens wanted to come down and see Convertors. I showed 'em around. There wasn't much to see and the tour probably lasted 15 minutes. We were standing out in the middle of the production floor and Jack Kimberly turned to Wright and asked, 'When did I authorize this operation?'

"I'd never seen a man turn gray, but Wright turned absolutely gray.

"I explained the problem with Ruby. I said Convertors was a good operation, profitable. I said Kimberly-Stevens should take it over and run it and earn some money, since they were struggling. Over drinks that night, Jack Kimberly and Bob Stevens decided, no, they were base-material suppliers, not converters, and they wouldn't compete with their customers.

"So, they decided to sell Convertors.

"I called the American Hospital executive, who flew in and said, 'I'll buy the operation tomorrow. I want the name, I want everything.'

"By the way, Convertors is one of the largest departments in Baxter today—they took over American Hospital—but even before they did, Convertors was their most profitable operation.

"Later, I got called over to an executive committee meeting. Unbeknownst to me, Jack Kimberly had called

Darwin in and given him hell for setting up this corporation. I was called in and Kimberly wanted to know, 'How much money did we lose?'

"I said, 'Actually we made money'.

"'I don't believe it!' He demanded an audit of the books. Actually, we made so much money that I was paying off some of my nonwovens research. I guess we had thirty-, forty-thousand dollars down in the bank in Oshkosh."

"What did you learn from Convertors?" I asked.

"I learned how to kite checks," Bill laughed. "I learned that if you want to do something and do it well and fast and efficiently, you do it outside of the major organization. I learned it isn't that tough to start a company. I learned about cash flow, a lot about how a business operates, the little things that you don't think of when you're in a big company. I guess it was my first lesson in the internal workings of a corporation."

Lanny rummaged through a file on the table, plucked out a Xerox copy of an official-looking document. It was the Entrepreneur's Award, voted by Kimberly-Clark's board of directors when Bill retired in 1988:

"WHEREAS, throughout almost 40 years of service William G. (Bill) Wilson has been known to many of his colleagues as a human idea machine; and...

"WHEREAS, he has proven himself to be not only a truly innovative thinker, but also a stimulator of innovative thinking in others—a person who challenged his cohorts to question the status quo and to look at things in a new light; and...

"WHEREAS, some 20 years ago, when nonwoven materials and processes were in their infancy, Bill's far-sighted concepts helped others see the potential greatness of these multi-use synthetic fibers; and...

"WHEREAS, nonwoven materials, in one form or another, now are used in products that account for more than 40 percent of Kimberly-Clark revenues...."

"Interesting: they didn't use the words 'Lying, stealing and cheating' in that resolution," I said.

Back to the '60s: Wilson had dodged the bullet with Convertors, but his efforts to drag Kimberly-Clark into the health-care business had been frustrated, perhaps fatally. Then, his career took a strange detour. And that detour put a new, sharp edge on the maverick's most essential tool.

"While I was director of New Products I pestered the executive group that they wouldn't know another Kleenex if it hit 'em right in the face," said Bill, grinning at the recollection.

"My example was an outfit that met with K-C's top physicist, Deke Davis, and asked for some help solving a problem. Deke worked on it for a week or so and solved it. Then he went to the head of K-C research and said,

'This little outfit has a pretty good idea here. Why doesn't Kimberly buy 'em?'

"It was presented to the executives and they weren't interested. This little outfit was called the Haloid Corporation. You know it as Xerox. I kept throwing things like that at them.

"So Bill Kellett (*K-C's president*) threw this back at me. He said, 'You've been pestering us, but we don't think you're a businessman. Maybe a good researcher, maybe a good technical guy, but we don't think you know one-two-three about business. So we're gonna give you this business called Industrial Wadding. Ten people over the last 15 years have tried to make something out of this area and nobody's succeeded. So, if you fail it won't be a black mark against you.'"

Bill, of course, said yes.

"I got industrial wadding, then wipes. Went from just under a million dollars in sales and almost nothing in profits to generating a hundred-thousand dollars in profits. In that group was a little business called industrial wipes, 'Kimwipes,' and in another six months we had it over a million dollars in sales and around $450,000 in profit. Fantastic.

"When they saw this, they said, 'Jeez, if Wilson can do this we'll give him Kotex vending, that's a dog. We'll give him the Marvelon business, a dog. We'll give him the foam business over here, that's a dog.' So I kept getting all these dogs dumped on me, and every three months I had to sit down with my key guys and say, 'What the hell business are we in?'"

"It's not only mavericks who are misfits, it's products that, quote, mis-fit, because they don't fit into some box of core competency," Lanny interjected. "Management consultants in the late '80s and '90s made a potful of money 'refocusing.' They went through corporations refocusing them on their core competencies and core disciplines. But the power of the maverick is that he can find what doesn't fit. What's outside the core."

"In my mind, we were a little conglomerate," Bill continued. "When I got the Kotex hospital maternity pad, we all said, Ahhhhh—we're legitimate. Now we can go into hospitals. And what have we got? A whole host of hospital products we've been quietly developing.

"By that time, I was selling a scrim-reinforced material to American Hospital and to Johnson & Johnson, and I was creaming the profit off and taking it over here and investing it to get us into the hospital business. It never went to the bottom line..."

"You *diverted* it?" I asked, not wanting to use a rougher-sounding word.

"He stole it fair and square," Lanny giggled.

"No. I just didn't tell 'em!" Bill said, sounding not the least bit defensive. "Because I was over there in Wadding, I was a legitimate profit center. And when you throw all this together and send it upstairs as one lump sum, they don't know how much is for wipes or for wadding. Hell, I was making an indecent profit off of wipes, I never got less than forty-percent profit. Even after I made wipes pay for a lot of other overheads, I still had a profit. All top management looked at was the total sales and the profit—they never asked more questions.

"Why the hell muddy it up? They had bigger problems. I was just a few million dollars. The fact I had collected a lot of businesses meant that I could hide things very easily. So the lying, cheating, stealing thing was a cinch."

"Lying interests me," said Lanny, like a scientist discovering a new species. "Truth comes in many forms. It can be precise, or it can be aimed at getting something done."

"But... *lying*," I said, still a little unnerved by the concept—and its consequences.

"Mostly they were half-truths." But Bill didn't look the least bit guilty. "I was 'dumping the basket' to see what would excite people. When I was in research, the scientists were upset because I was never technically correct in what I would communicate to upper management. They kept saying, 'You aren't telling the truth; this is not scientifically correct.' And I'd say, 'Forget it. Do you want to go ahead with this program, want to get some money for it or not? I know how to communicate this so management will give you the money.' The purpose of communication isn't agreement but progress."

"And cheating," added Lanny, "is a matter of breaking the rules so you can change them. So you can invent new rules. The maverick steals from the present, as Bill did with the health care initiative, for the benefit of the future."

Not the future of the quarterly stock price but the deep future, where companies that have lost sight of renewal (or as Lanny put it, "freshness") inevitably die.

FENCE-CUTTERS.

There were other tools, as we began to "graze" in the maverick metaphor. One tool was suggested by a Wilson quip: "One of my bosses used to call me an iconoclast. He said, 'Wilson, I spend half my time going around mending fences that you knock down.'"

"So, maybe the maverick's got a pair of wire-cutters in that saddlebag," I said. "The maverick cuts fences."

"Innovations," Lanny intoned, "are a function of what happens when boundaries that are constructed by convention or perception are exposed and crossed and something new is learned in the crossing. This is the essence of the maverick. Someone who crosses boundaries, commandeers the learning that the crossing produces and then makes it available to create something new."

"Right," I grinned.

Bill had a ready example of fence-cutting and border-crossing. It went back to 1946, his first Kimberly-Clark job, a posting at K-C's Spruce Falls mill at Kapuscasing, Ontario. (Having lived in Oregon, I knew the reality of mill towns to be far from charming.) His first big job assignment from the mill's assistant manager, Guy Minard, a man himself headed for bigger things at K-C, was to "go and investigate wood."

It seemed an odd request: wasn't the mill's very essence wood? But there were two divisions operating out there: Mill, which processed the logs; and Woodlands, which cut them down. They were entirely separate kingdoms.

"With a wall between them," said Bill. "The Mill manager and the Woodlands manager were co-equal and they reported to different people down in Neenah. Separate as can be. The communication between them was terrible."

It sounded depressingly similar to my experience in the newspaper world—the fabled wall between "church" (editorial) and "state" (the wretches who sold advertising). One crossed that wall at great professional peril.

"So Minard flipped you over that wall," I said. "One day, you just show up..."

"I asked them to teach me about wood. And they agreed. I went out in the spring, summer, winter; saw how they cut the timber; how they brought it to the banks of the river; how they piled it on the ice; how they drove it down the river after the freshet; how they did all of these various things. So I got to know not only the top people in Woodlands, but the next layer and the next layer down, by working with these guys.

"Let me jump a bit. All us young engineers would sit around a big table in the dining room of the company's hotel and we would talk about what we were working on. And one fellow kind of bragged that he had just signed a contract for $560-thousand to mechanically unload wood.

"I said,'That's great, but within twelve months there isn't going to be any wood delivered that way.'

"He said, 'What do you mean? Wood's always been delivered that way!'

"I said, 'Don't ask me, go over to Woodlands and ask them.'

"The next day, we had a big summit conference. Engineering presented their plans and the Woodlands guys said, 'Yeah, that's probably gonna work.'

"The Mill engineer says, 'Bill tells us there won't be any wood coming in that way.'

"And the Woodlands guy says, 'That's right.'

"They had never talked to one another. We would have built that half-million dollar thing and it'd be sitting there to this day."

As I listened to the stories, a picture emerged: Wilson the hick from upcountry Ontario emerging as a fast-moving player with scant regard for boundaries and a brief from management to cut through them; who could take a weirdly unfocused set of marching orders—"Find out about wood"—and turn that into a way to learn and to *do*.

And there was a hint of something else: the maverick's puckish willingness to tweak conventional wisdom, the joy of dropping a water balloon on conventional thinking.

Bill quickly became known as an unorthodox problem-solver. When ordered to find out why the mill's cranes were breaking down regularly, he hit on the novel idea of asking the crane operators to solve the problem (this, 40-odd years before "empowerment").

He devised a mechanical log unloader that was vastly more efficient—and cost all of fifty bucks. He reduced the log inventory by $3-million, long before "just in time." Reduced the wood-chipping operation's staffing from 12 workers to one.

Within two years, he had worked himself out of the mill and down to corporate headquarters where he took a seat as a very junior apparatchik in the technical planning bureaucracy. It was a typical blue-suit-and-white-shirt job where underlings were expected to keep their mouths shut. But, as we know, Bill was a *maverick*.

BRAKES.

When a fat file detailing plans for a mill's routine equipment-request landed on Bill's desk, he didn't rubber-stamp it. Instead, true to the definition of a maverick as "one who does the unexpected and goes against conventional wisdom wherever it is found," he rebelled.

"They were going to replace two sulfur burners, which were towers about three stories tall," said Bill. (Papermaking in those years used vast quantities of sulfuric acid, which is one reason older books turn yellow and brittle). "I went over to the chemical engineers. A fellow named Jim Shipman was in charge of the lab. I said, 'Here's what they're going to do. It's going to cost about a half-million dollars. There ought to be a better way.'"

"Shipman said, 'Burning is only time, temperature and turbulence.'

"'What does that mean?'

"'If you want to shorten the time—which the big chamber gives you—you've got to increase the temperature and the turbulence.'

"'How do you do that?'

"He said, 'By building it like a jet engine.'"

Wilson and Shipman (another rising star in Kimberly-Clark) built a prototype out of a 14-inch sewer pipe in back of the research department.

"And the damned thing worked."

Bill refused to sign the mill's request. And he convinced his boss not to sign, either. This, of course, prompted an angry meeting with the mill engineers.

Shipman's pitch—garnished by the fact that he had worked during World War II developing the ramjet engine—swayed the mill people. Half way: They authorized one of the new-fangled pipes and built a second unit in the traditional style.

"Shipman and I went to start it up. The acid-maker usually came in at midnight so that by eight o'clock in the morning the acid would be up to strength to cook the pulp.

"About ten minutes after we fired up the new unit, the acid-maker pulled me aside and whispered, 'We're up to full strength on the acid.'

"I said, 'So soon? Hell, we just got started. Let's dump it and re-do it.'

"Ten minutes later, same thing happens. Tanks are all full. And we're not past twelve-thirty.

"And, of course they were mad as hell with me because I let them build that one old unit that didn't give them the same results."

TELLING A STORY THAT'S NEVER FINISHED.

"What other tools does the maverick have in his saddlebags?" Lanny asked

"Bill's *stories*?" I wondered.

"Story-telling is transformative and interpretive," said Lanny after a second's thought, "and that's what the maverick knows. The maverick uses story-telling as a transformative tool. Forging the future means living where story and reality intersect."

"Uhhh, right," I said. I reminded myself that Lanny had been trained as a theologian.

"The story-teller is someone who shows up and helps people get out of the funk of the present and into the future," said Lanny, on a roll. "And a story is a great vehicle for doing that because it carries people and lifts them up—it's redemptive. So the maverick's game is to keep the story going."

"A story is certainly a hell of a lot easier to listen to than some dry report," I said. "And great stories teach; they reach some new insight about the human condition."

"Stories are lies in the service of a higher reality," said Lanny. "That's why Bill was mistrusted by some folks around K-C."

"Great stories also persuade the reader to suspend disbelief," I said.

"And doing that is really the only way for people in the organization's operating world—reality—to enter the development world of innovation," Lanny added. "The world of imagination.

"The irony," he added, "is that stories are not 'businesslike.' Stories are not Wall Street. Tables and numbers and charts are business, right?"

"Supposedly," said Bill. "But I always got along well

with securities analysts because I told them stories. What the hell do you tell an analyst when you're in charge of new products? You don't spill your guts to 'em."

Lanny giggled. "An analyst talking to someone in new products is like a match held up to gasoline."

"So I told 'em stories," said Bill. "And they were fascinated."

"What were the stories?" I asked.

"They were mostly about failure. Because you can't do harm with failure, you know."

"Maybe that's the key to the maverick's resilience," I mused, his ability to endure failure—indeed, to seemingly court it." Failure makes a hell of a plot point, doesn't it?"

"And to tell stories," added Lanny, "you need characters. Bringing people together—collecting them—is like creating a story. People aren't 'resources,' but characters."

"And they don't all have to be heroes; in fact you *need* villains," I said.

"The head of consumer testing would destroy whatever new products we brought to him," said Bill. "But, gradually, I began to recognize that he was our greatest asset because he would show us exactly where the problems were and we could then leverage that knowledge. Once you've got that leverage, then you've got real power."

TNT; EMPTY THREATS; CALCULATED STUPIDITY.

Gradually, as we talked, we began adding more tools, large and small, all unconventional, to the maverick's saddlebag. One, harking back to Bill's time deep inside the Ontario gold mines, was "TNT."

"If you've got a big project going in a certain direction," Bill grinned, "it's like an ocean liner, trying to turn the damned thing around. But when you see you're going to run into an iceberg, when you see you won't be able to sell it, it'll be killed, that's when you blow the damned thing up—you shatter the project, see what you've got, rethink it, look at the pieces that are assets, what are the best ways to capitalize on them.

"If you can say, This piece belongs way over here, and this piece over there—pretty soon you've disassembled it. But each individual who had a part of it still has a part, except they're in a different place, reporting to a different person, different people surrounding them."

"You blow it up to save it," I said.

"The maverick uses another tool," said Bill. "Empty threats."

Skritch-skritch: the word went up on the paper.

"We developed a number of things in the O-C group in the '50s" said Bill. "The difficulty was transfer, having somebody pick it up. For two years we struggled with that."

"Essentially the 'Not-Invented-Here' syndrome," I said.

"Sure. Here I am, supposedly trying to develop something to make the professionals in research more creative and those guys said, 'Hell, we're creative as can be.'

"But in fact it *did* make the professionals more creative. They weren't using any of the techniques we were developing but, nonetheless, they got off their asses and started to do something. They produced a hell of a lot more. Y'know, competition is a great thing.

"When I worked for Bill in Innovation Management," Lanny interjected, "we had our own projects that we were betting on, but there were always projects that belonged to somebody else at K-C and Bill wanted us to work on those, too.

"At one point we said, 'Bill, we can't do our own (projects) and work on somebody else's project. What do you want? Do you want us to be effective or do you want us to be productive?"

"And he said, 'Effective.'

"We didn't fully appreciate—I certainly didn't—until later that he what he was asking us to do was absolutely deliberate. He had learned with his previous experience that if you don't work on other people's projects, if you don't support their ownership when it comes your time you won't get their support. And you'll have fostered an attitude that others perceived you to be elitist."

That's why 20 years after the O-C group, as vice president of Exploratory Projects and then vice president of Innovation Management, Bill approached selling his projects far differently: "We deliberately left things out, things that we knew could be done better.

"We would design stupidity into the product so the organization people would immediately start to 'improve' what we had done. Now they're sucked in; they're getting over the Not-Invented-Here syndrome because they're putting something of their own into it."

MORPHING.

"All of this suggests to me that the maverick lives in two different zones," said Lanny. "One is in reserve and one is active. When they're in reserve, they're looking for problems. When they're active, they're looking for solutions. In other words, the maverick morphs. The maverick is a chameleon."

"A maverick can play many roles," said Bill. "And he doesn't always play the role of the maverick. A maverick can transform himself depending on the situation. I could be either a Canadian or an American—whatever worked."

"It's not just that the maverick morphs," I said, "but that the maverick moves in relation to projects and people in a very unique way. The maverick doesn't always have to be at the head of the pack. It's what Lanny told me, Bill—that you were somewhere in the vicinity of success, but not necessarily at the center."

"That's true," said Wilson. He looked almost sheepish, as though I had caught him out.

"You were perfectly willing to use people in a rather calculated way," I said, although I meant it less as an indictment than an insight.

"I suppose I played a mentoring role; I played the role of sponsor at times; at times I'd lead and then, if there were people willing to grab things and run, all I would do is run interference for them."

There was a momentary silence. We stared into the figurative saddlebags that we had filled with our collection of unorthodox—but *very* sharp-edged tools:

Lying, stealing, cheating.
Collecting.
Keeping the story going.
Applying brakes.
TNT.
Empty threats.
Calculated stupidity.
Morphing.

"Tough tools," I muttered. "Tough to use without lopping off one of your fingers."

Lanny and Bill agreed. It pointed toward the dilemmas in the maverick's unique role. Lanny drew a line down the center of a big sheet of paper and we listed the conflicts built into the maverick's role:

Freedom vs. responsibility.
Contribute to the organization vs. being true to yourself.
Using tools vs. becoming captive to them.
Transcending the rules vs. ignoring the rules.
Doesn't care what others think vs. working in a group.
Respecting prior efforts vs. using the past to excuse inaction.

It was a tightrope, strung across a deep chasm. Alligators (many wearing pin-striped suits) waited lazily at the bottom, sure in the knowledge that, one fine day, the tightrope walker would surely slip.

Bill, I realized, had spent 42 years on and off that rope. He had crossed the chasm dozens of times. It had been a remarkable performance. But now a new thought intruded:

Had he slipped? And what had happened when he hit bottom?

If everyone is thinking alike,
then someone isn't thinking.

Gen. George S. Patton

5.
Free Range.

WHERE THE MAVERICK ROAMS.

We seemed to have hit a dead-end. We had "pinned the specimen to the card"—but, to do that, we had immobilized the maverick. Now it was time to figure out where the maverick moved, how he moved.

"Let's go back to the metaphor," Lanny prompted.

"Samuel Maverick helped to create the Texas Republic, the land was in a transitional stage," I mused.

"They called it free range," added Lanny.

"Free range was a transitional period from non-ownership to 'let's measure it, put lines on it, dominate it,' Free range doesn't work if you've got a bunch of farmers out there.

"So, it's a very, very brief moment in American history. Yet it's a moment that's very potent in terms of the American self-image and imagination. It's John Ford and the Duke and 'Lonesome Dove.' It's youthful innocence. The promise of a map with blank spaces. The wow! you get from glimpsing the future."

"The maverick is obsessed by searching for the future," said Bill.

"Free range isn't under control," I said. "It changes depending on the other animals that are wandering around. It shifts from hour to hour, minute to minute."

Now Lanny started turning my meanderings into hard-edged concepts: Free range is an area that's rich with the potential for corporate growth and innovation. By being "unbranded," the maverick is able to cut across both internal and external borders, bringing people and ideas together. Therefore, "the maverick is less interested in political and organizational boundaries. The maverick is interested in topography..."

"...the lay of the land..." said Bill.

"Right—the topography of markets and technology. And yet, unlike the heretic, who flies in the face of these boundaries, the maverick understands that boundaries are strictly virtual; they're not real. So, the maverick is someone who can live in two worlds at the same time. He's smart enough to know that his access to resources must be negotiated with the formal power structure, which is the virtual world of boundaries and rules..."

"...but the maverick can move through those boundaries," I added.

"There are many ways to cross a border," said Lanny. "Walter Paul kept going back and forth on the border between civilization and the wilderness. Bill's a Canadian; he's an American who lived on European soil. When you're a foreigner you're much more aware of two things: the strangeness of the land that you're in and the strangeness of your own normative standards."

"'Make it strange,' was a key to synectics and the invention process," said Bill.

"So, free range is a place where the rules are being

formed and re-formed," said Lanny. "Two things are battling it out—liberation versus domestication. And that's what the free range is about. It's a place of conflict."

"And the maverick collects conflict," Bill said.

It reminded me of Bill's stint, in the late '50s, as head of the Operational Creativity Group. His White Russian émigré, Serge Bouderline (the fellow who nonplussed the Personnel people by asking to live in the Appleton slums), created something called "The Trend Room." It was a conference room lined with cork; anyone—it made

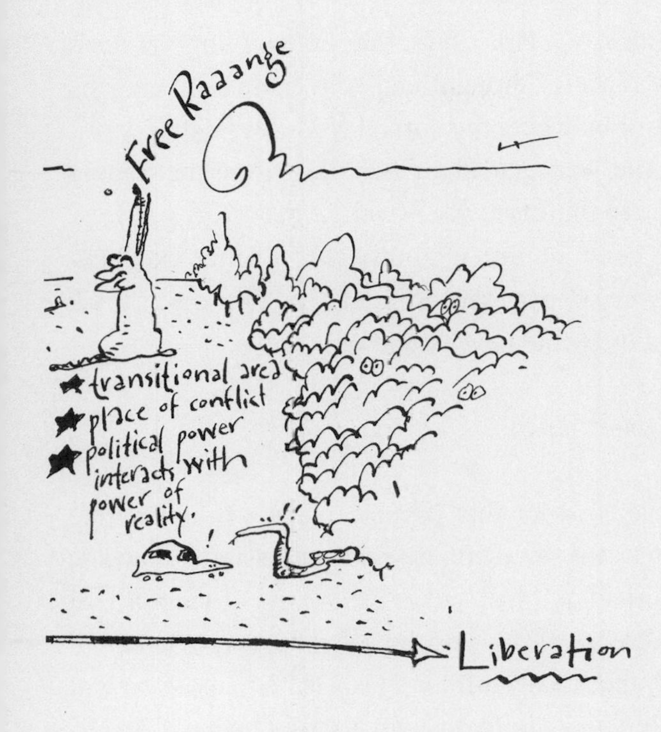

no difference whether they were inside or outside the O-C group—could post anything on its walls that seemed interesting, sparkled with a potential idea, evoked a chuckle or a snort of outrage. Soon the room was lined with hundreds of photos, clippings, scraps and bits of ephemera, a collage that, weirdly, started to make sense. And then, just as quickly, changed, morphed, into something entirely different. Then morphed again.

The room, I realized, was one of Bill's early versions of free range, long before we had named it. It was a room inside Kimberly-Clark's headquarters building yet apart from it; a place of thought and subversion, dreams and wishes. A room where the normal K-C rules didn't apply. Once people went into the room, they gave themselves permission to think and act… well, *differently*.

"Serge could go into a fantasy world better than anyone I've ever known," said Bill quietly. "One day, I think he went in there and never came out."

MAPPING FREE RANGE.

I was curious about this psychic place we called free range: What was out there, beyond cactus and outlaws?

As it turned out, Bill had drawn a kind of map of free range—back in 1984—just one of the many charts and grids and graphs that stuff his files. He had presented it at a Kimberly-Clark conference for R-and-D people. Fortunately, it had been videotaped.

That night, we popped it in Bill's tape player and opened a sort of time capsule.There was Bill—over a decade younger, hair darker—but essentially unchanged. He sat on a stage in a Kimberly-Clark auditorium with a protégé, Dave Lincoln (since retired), who went back to Bill's days in New Products. As always, Bill told "anecdotes," as Lincoln called them.

I had heard many of them before, damn near word-for-word.

Then the camera swung over to a slide projected as Bill made a point. It looked like this:

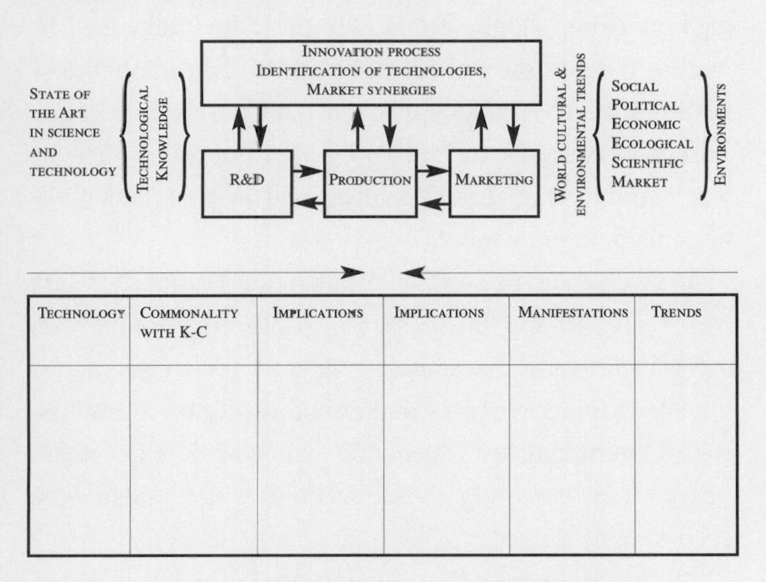

It seemed daunting at first, but as Bill talked on the tape, it became clear that this was his diagram of what we were now calling free range—the territory that exists outside the corporate fence.

"Over here on the left is technology," said Bill on the tape. "You keep in touch with the cutting-edge trends in electronics, energy, robotics, biotechnology—*everything*." On the right side of the chart, "You keep in touch with the trends that are going on throughout society. Social, political, economic, ecological."

Bill remarked that he kept a file for each of the topics

that he tracked—a paper version of the "Trends Room"—full of clippings, notes, books, scientific papers, patent applications. As the file thickened, he would ponder the emerging trend's "commonalities" with Kimberly-Clark's particular business skills. Which, in turn, went back to Bill's pregnant question when he was running Industrial Wadding and Wipes: "What the hell business are we in?"

I recalled his toss-off comment that Kimberly-Clark was really in the business of "preventing embarrassment," an insight that hadn't endeared him to the macho guys hacking down trees and transforming them into tissue. Commonalities depended on where you stood. Maybe they were only visible when you were outside the corporate fence.

"I've discovered that once you have implications derived from technology trends and implications coming from social trends, you'll find that some implications from one side will match perfectly with implications from the other. What you're looking for is future technology, needs and wants of future markets, and where they fit," said the electronic Bill. Then, he added, "You put the innovation process on top."

Innovation, in Bill's scheme, wasn't limited to classic R-and-D, but included production and marketing. His chart portrayed a free-flowing process: back-and-forth, up-and-down, boundaries crossed and re-crossed with impunity. Just as a maverick travels through the organizational chart.

"The bottom line," said Lincoln, "has to do with making these connections and continuously collecting relevant and irrelevant information, putting it together, going for that fit. It's a way of life."

Then Bill told "anecdotes" about his forays into free range. One of them illustrated a phrase that I had heard from Lanny and the Synectics crew: "The problem as given versus the problem as understood."

I had always been a little puzzled by that phrase—a problem is a problem, right? When your boss drops a smelly puzzle on your desk, you go and try your damndest to do something—*anything!*—about it.

"The problem as given," said Lincoln to knowing chuckles from the researchers in the room, "has been developed, excruciated over and finally everybody signs off. But many times the problem that's talked about by the marketer or the business guy isn't really the problem at all. I'll give you an example.

"Kimberly-Clark's vice president for sales came to us and said, 'I have a cost problem with my cut sizes of fine paper at the Neenah and Munising mills.'

"The solution that we gave him two years later was a pair of consumer products for retail sales: Scribe and the Wordmaster paper lines. And we gave him a mechanism that avoided cut sheets altogether by selling small rolls that had been engineered to go on the back of Addresso-graph machines.

"The VP refused to accept those solutions even though they not only resolved his profit problems because we got a greater mark-up for these products, but they also gave him a lot more volume because they were new markets. He refused those because they weren't the problem he had given us. If we had been smarter in those days, we would have rephrased our understanding of the problem back to the sponsor and gotten his acceptance earlier."

Then Bill jumped in: When the vice president "turned us down, we went out and sold the (roll adapter patent) to Addressograph." And, as it turned out, the rolled paper was supplied by a Kimberly arch-rival, International Paper. "It was a considerable volume of paper," Bill added dryly.

But even though the paper-roll idea had been turned into cash (which Bill quietly funneled back into his non-wovens research), he wasn't willing to take no for an answer on Scribe and Wordmaster. In fact, he went back into the free range—in this case to the South Side of Chicago.

"We wanted more data. More facts. We set up a store. What are we going to put in the store besides writing paper? We decided to put some personal products in it. We put in some paperback books. Some toys. We put market-research people at the cash register and we got the names and addresses of people who bought things in our store because we ran all kinds of promotions and prizes."

As usual, Bill hadn't asked for permission to set up his very own convenience store. Nor did he have a budget.

"Basically what we had down in Chicago," said Lincoln, "was a retail laboratory that we were running for our own purposes. But because we needed all the other products to fill the shelves, we saw an opportunity to develop and generate information on a lot of other product categories."

"We did market research on paperback books," said Bill, looking naughty and pleased simultaneously. "We went over to Avon Books and they bought it. Then we went to Mattel Toys and did research on *their* products."

Meanwhile, he was learning a lot about retailing paper.

"We started to sell paper by the inch. We sold it by the pound. All sorts of different sizes and prices. We were trying to find out how people wanted to buy it. We found that it was 100 sheets that sold—price had nothing to do with it.

"Then we put Scribe and Wordmaster into Jewel Tea supermarkets. They made more profit on our four-foot section of shelving than anything else in the store."

"We moved to Jewel," said Lincoln with a guarded

chuckle, "and then a negative technique—preliminary disclosure to management—hit us."

Bill: "Our consumer sales force made a call at Jewel and the president said, 'Boy, this writing paper thing is absolutely terrific.'"

The vice president of consumer products—the same fellow who had already turned down Scribe and Wordmaster—was not amused.

"You can imagine what hit the fan," Bill grinned as nervous laughter rippled through the audience. "I was called on the carpet. I explained what we were doing. And Consumer Products took it over.

"But they didn't pay any attention to what we had learned in our original store—the basis for the success. They redid the market research with the advertising agency. They had a big rollout all over the West Coast. And it wasn't very successful.

"It so happened that there was a young man in training on the West Coast named Claudio Gonzalez, and when he went back to Mexico, he remembered Scribe and Wordmaster. He asked me what made it go. We gave him a copy of the original marketing report."

Lincoln jumped in: "And he listened to what made it go as opposed to what the consumer division had done. They tried to refine it under their methods—but when you get a success you should let it live like it wants to live—and that's why Scribe and Wordmaster has been a mainstay of the Mexican operation for the last twenty-five years." (Gonzalez became chairman of the board of Kimberly-Clark de Mexico in 1973 and joined the K-C Board in 1976.)

Bill summed up: "You need courage. You come to a fork in the road; the easy thing is to do nothing. The easy thing is to ask someone else to make the decision for you. The tougher thing is to go out there and *do* something. If you're convinced that this is a good idea, that it's a good product, that it will work—stick with it."

The crowd's applause at the end of the program was sincere enough—but, I wondered, how many in that room had *heard* Bill? How many had cut the fence and sought the loneliness of the free range? It was a new question, worth filing away for future reference: What was Bill's legacy at K-C? Had he left behind protégés? If so, had they, too, found a way to cut through the fence?

A SAFARI ONTO FREE RANGE.

Some time after the Tucson session broke up, Lanny sent me a note via e-mail. He had been thinking about his experiences with Bill—experiences, he now realized, that represented excursions into that psychic space that we had dubbed free range.

"I recall the time that Bill sent me to a conference at the Aspen Institute. The conference was a small and intimate affair. Its subject matter was media—which didn't seem to have anything to do with Kimberly-Clark's product categories, past, present or, conceivably, in the future.

"Bill told me to go and listen to what the experts were arguing about. He believed this would tell us not *what* was coming, but *where* change would be occurring.

"Reluctantly and resentfully I went. There was a guy from some outfit I had never heard of—Industrial Light and Magic. What I heard the experts arguing about was something called 'interactivity.' This, mind you, was in 1982. Not many had even heard of the Internet, or interactive TV or video games.

"In hindsight, it's scary how accessible the future (free range in a time dimension) really is with Bill's approach of finding the experts in a field and listening to what they are arguing about (i.e., that field's free range).

"Bill would take excursions frequently—literally and figuratively—as a way of exploring the free range of ideas, trends, new management techniques, etc.

"Even if we could not apply it successfully, it was still considered worthwhile to have made these excursions into the free range because of the freshness and energy these trips brought to the group."

All good things were at
one time bad things; every
original sin has developed
into an original virtue.

Friedrich Nietzsche

6.
Pasture.

Mavericks get dinged by organizations because they don't want to own something.

CUTTING THE FENCE.

When the maverick cuts through the fence, to follow our metaphor, he is also leaving some place behind, just as the O-C types left the corporate world when they disappeared into The Trend Room.

So—what was that place?

"Pasture," Lanny said. "It's the antithesis of free range: you have a farm, and there's a border, a fence. The corporation frequently conceives of itself as a farmer would—it builds a fence around itself."

"Pasture is gated," said Bill. "Pasture animals don't want to cut the fence and go outside. They want to control the gate. Who gets in. Who gets out."

"Only the maverick knows how to make part of the range a pasture,"he continued. "You take part of the range—OK, I'm done with this part now, I don't need to tramp it anymore, I know all about it: you guys turn it into pasture."

"If you follow this analogy," said Lanny, "when a corporation patents something, they're turning free range into pastureland. And they're doing that in terms of brands, trademarks, distribution, market penetration.

"It goes back to Bill's story about the Tomahawk conspiracy. The people at Bill's secret meeting said, 'We know if K-C is going to grow, it's going to have to do it on the free range.' They did two things: They declared what part of the free range they would grow Kimberly-Clark into—health care."

"We started to put a border around it," said Bill. "We knew that eventually we would develop it into a pasture."

"The other thing you did," said Lanny, "is you didn't *call* it a pasture. It was covert. You were smart enough to know that the new would be rejected."

" As it was," said Bill.

MAVERICKS AND FARMERS.

"So, how does the maverick get an innovation from the free range, back into the pasture?" Lanny asked. "How do you bring it into the organization?"

"To use the pasture analogy," I said, "if you bring a coyote into the pasture, the guard dogs are going to rip it to shreds. As they should."

"So the maverick's got to have a partner in the pasture," said Lanny. "Whether it's the CEO or manager or whoever. Because what the maverick brings back into the pasture is both disruptive and promising.

"You'd think, at face value, that the maverick is only interested in free range…liberation," said Lanny. "But I think the maverick is actually interested—and what distinguishes the maverick from the entrepreneur—is a loyalty and affinity to what's going on in the pasture. The maverick wants to renew the organization's entrepreneurial roots, because by doing so, the maverick earns more freedom— more freedom, arguably, than the entrepreneur

"So our message to the CEO is: when you want to expand the pasture, you need to be able to play on the free range. You don't want to pick an outlaw to do this, because you can't trust 'em. A scout is an interesting alternative, but they're not interested in domestication. They're interested in moving on.

"The maverick, however, is the one you want. You need to find your maverick."

WHY FREE RANGE ISN'T FOR SALE.

The idea of free range vs. pasture poses a question: Why not simply buy the freshest ideas and innovations, as opposed to going through the arduous task of developing innovation internally? A few months after our Tucson meeting, Lanny was still pondering that question (and beginning to form an answer) in this piece from his *Innovating Perspectives* newsletter:

The Quiet Alternative

> "Acquisitions grab headlines; internal new product and business development efforts do not. Which is better?

"A recent article in the *Wall Street Journal* (October 12, 1998) cited studies which concluded that a slight majority of new acquisitions do not work. Ironically, this is apparently becoming accepted wisdom in investment banking circles. Both A.T. Kearney and Mercer Management Consulting found that almost 60% of acquisitions did not 'add value,' as defined by share price after the deal and indexed to the industry's performance.

"In another study using similar measures, J.P. Morgan found that not quite 50% of acquisitions did not add value after three years. Reasons for the failures (or unmet expectations) included paying too high a premium in the deal and underestimating the requirements of successfully integrating the acquired company.

"Some may conclude from these studies that to make a deal work—i.e., to add value—one needs not only to pay the right price but be prepared for a significant effort (and cost) to integrate the acquisition. Another conclusion, however, seems reasonable as well—consider internal development of what is being sought from the acquisition. In other words, instead of looking to 'add value' by means of an acquisition, create value by means of internal development efforts.

"In the May 18, 1998, issue of *Forbes* magazine,

John Rutledge takes up the question from his own personal perspective. 'Should [we] develop a new product inside or acquire a company that can design, manufacture and distribute the product?' Rutledge suggests that to answer this question a thorough analysis of both alternatives is required. The answer resides in a comparison of the resulting cash flow implications from which one can determine which option will increase the intrinsic value of the company.

"However, financial analysis alone will not produce an answer that you can trust. This mistake is often made—relying on financial people to do the comparative analysis. There are too many variables that are not easily quantifiable. Instead of arguing about the right number for the cost of capital, what is needed is for the various managers who will be involved, irrespective of whether the decision is to make or buy, to interact as much as possible in developing five-year financial projections for each alternative.

"In Rutledge's experience, while the 'buy' alternative looked attractive, a closer look at the 'make' alternative revealed a significantly higher reward—increasing the value of the company three times more than the 'buy' alternative.

Important to note, however, is the fact that in Rutledge's example, greater rewards required patience.

"Can we extrapolate from this experience to all other 'make or buy' decisions? Perhaps not. Each may require its own specific case-by-case comparative analysis. However, it should cause us to stop and consider the possibility—or is it probability—of higher rewards from choosing the path of internal development instead of acquisition."

When he sent me the clipping, Lanny wrote the following on the margin: "Acquiring another pasture is one approach. Developing or acquiring a piece of the free range is another. Cisco Systems seems to be doing the latter, with much more success than companies that do the former."

Mavericks vs. 'The People Who Know One Thing.'

Mid-afternoon: My brain was beginning to feel a little fuzzy. Bill must have felt the vibe, for he suggested that we pile into his van.

"Let's go see Leo," he said, striding toward the door.

As we maneuvered through Tucson's desert-girded streets, Bill explained that Leo Shapiro was one of his oldest friends. They had met during Bill's New Product days and had remained close ever since. In fact, they got together with another pal at regular intervals to toss one of their personal or professional problems on the table, then brainstorm possible solutions. One of those sessions had led Leo, founder of Chicago-based Leo Shapiro and Associates, to aggregate his firm's market-research data—everything from private school preferences to studies of right- and left-handedness—and bundle the insights for the securities industry, where it had been richly valued and rewarded.

Bill called Shapiro a marketing genius: "Leo has an uncanny ability to hear a product. Not what people *say* about it, because people—you show them a new product and they want to say something positive about it; they want to tell you what you want to hear. Leo can hear the things you don't want to hear."

We pulled into the driveway of a brick-faced condo. Bill rang the bell and Leo's wife, Virginia, answered the door. We stepped inside. The house was eerily empty—she explained they were renting it while looking for a permanent place here in the desert.

"Over here, Bill!" called a commanding voice. We followed it into the living room. Plastic patio furniture sat grouped around a big bed where Leo Shapiro lay flat on his back, a pajama shirt flopped open on a muscular chest. But, under a thin coverlet, his legs were alarmingly thin; twigs that looked as if they could snap like kindling. A pair of crutches leaned against the bed's headboard.

"I hope you don't mind if I don't get up," Leo said, explaining that he had contracted polio as a child, had recovered, but now was suffering post-polio syndrome, a nasty rebound in which muscles seem to "remember" the original affliction.

Leo raised his arm and Lanny and I shook his hand. I looked down into the face of a biblical prophet—wise, piercing eyes set in a deeply-lined countenance that a portrait sculptor would yearn to portray in bronze.

Bill told Leo that Lanny and I were in Tucson to work on the book—as yet untitled, formless. Leo nodded. He and Bill had been talking about it. Then, without prompting, he began a rambling, utterly fascinating, occasionally opaque rapid-fire monologue that quickly outran my note-taking: one-liners, aphorisms, jokes—and I remembered what Bill had said on the way over: "At first what Leo says might not make any sense, but in a day or two you'll get it."

"I wouldn't call Bill a maverick," said Leo, as I leaned forward to catch the shadow of an ironic smile drifting across his face's craggy landscape. "I'd call him *unusual.*"

Bill laughed. Then Leo said something that, at the time, struck me as a non sequitur but ultimately sent our inquiry spiraling off into a whole new direction.

"Bill could never become Kimberly-Clark's CEO, but he could never be fired."

But before I could form a question about that, Leo was soaring off on another vector. "Your book's an adventure in living," he said. "It's about how to stay fresh in the afternoon of ideas, life, markets. It's a book about what you would do if you were starting over, rather than retrofitting the present to the past...

"The process of organizational change parallels personal change—you can't have one without the other. Nothing happens in a business without relationships.

"If you don't know where you're going, any road will take you there. Bill, on the other hand, knew where he was going and would allow the group to take him there.

"Many people get ahead (in an organization) by focusing on one thing—they're not distracted by ideas. They're the people who know one thing; they're focused on career management. All 'career management' is in conflict with corporate management.

"Mavericks don't get ahead because they have more than one idea. They're focused on corporate renewal."

SURPRISES.

"I'm in a strange business," said Leo, taking the monologue off on yet another tangent. "I get hired to find surprises by companies, governments, groups of people whose success depends on influencing more people than they can reach individually. When I come back and deliver the surprise, it's a traumatic experience for the client. When I bring a surprise to someone, I am turning that person into an infant. He or she has spent his entire life, from the age of nine days onward, to avoiding surprises.

"When something suddenly disturbs them, they have to reject it until they can incorporate it. And so they cry, just like a baby. It's unpleasant.

"We are living in a society where people have a very rigid view of themselves and their relationship to the world and they've lost the plasticity of children. Think how nice it would be if you could learn as fast as a newborn. The trick is to mature in a fashion that retains your ability to adapt to reality as a child does. Why do people resist alternative views? Why do they resist surprises? It's because it's a challenge to their adulthood. So, this book is about growing up."

"Growing up?" I wondered out loud. *Hey! This is a biz book, Leo!*

"The thing that is most characteristic of Bill is his capacity to accept alternative points of view. And contradictions. And live with them. So, this book would serve people by telling them how wonderful it is to find disagreements. To find things that they *don't* know.

"Let's take an event that might be regarded as seminal and interpret it in terms of being a mature person who accepts reality. Let's talk about the diaper."

Ahhh, yes; the diaper!

I recalled that Lanny had said something vague about Bill's role in creating the disposable diaper—a godsend to parents, as I knew from direct experience with my daughter decades before. And so I echoed the magic words: "Disposable diaper," to interrupt Leo's free-association flow. It worked; the river of thought was diverted. And we went back, to the late '50s, when Leo and Bill were young corporate warriors.

"The first reality," said Leo, "was that nobody wanted a disposable diaper. They wanted a diaper that *works*. That's a very strange reality. And Bill was able to accept it."

Bill jumped in. "Now, no woman ever said that—but this is how Leo hears a product."

"So, if cloth diapers are no damned good, what do you do?" Leo asked. "You try to invent a better diaper and you don't worry about marketing and that's what Bill did. He didn't say build me a diaper that costs this and does that. He said 'What would a good diaper look like, what would it be like?' Now let's keep going. You now have a diaper and it costs a dollar-seventy-five a copy. Bill accepts that. No despair."

Bill jumped back into the dialogue: "We started making test diapers. It was during this period that Dick Loescher and I went over to a show-and-tell at the executive committee—Jack Kimberly, chairman of the board; Kellett, the president; the vice presidents of the major areas. I talked about the work we were doing with the diaper.

"Jack Kimberly said, 'For thirty years we've tried to make a disposable diaper. Working on that is like sitting on a bridge tearing up hundred-dollar bills and throwing them in the water and watching them float downstream. I want all work on disposable diapers discontinued as of now.'

"So I quit talking about that. After the meeting, when we were walking back to our building, I said to Loescher, 'Dick, you know what we ought to do on diapers now...'

"Loescher stopped me and said, 'Bill, you got a direct order from the chairman of the board.'

"I said, 'From now on that project is called bandages.'"

Leo and Lanny chuckled at the recollection as I made a mental cross-reference—yup, it was classic lying, stealing and cheating.

Now Leo's voice echoed from the bed. "You must understand that there is a thing called bureaucratic reality—which is those things that people agree to accept as true—and there's an external reality. Unless you understand the bureaucratic reality and live within it you'll never accomplish anything. But unless you understand that it's a set of truths by agreement, you'll never be worth a damn in terms of changing anything."

And Leo illustrated his point by going back to the diaper's twisted history: "The first marketing test of the diaper in Grand Rapids, Michigan, was interrupted because it was selling so well that it went over budget. It killed the product for three years.

"The guy who stopped the test got promoted. Bureaucratic reality—deliver things on time and on budget. So how did Bill change the bureaucratic reality so it conformed more closely to the external reality?"

Bill jumped back into the conversation: "We were working in the health-care field, so I could finesse work, hide it, so this wasn't a complete out-and-out lie." (*But, as I recalled, this was work that Bill and the Tomahawk Group—his "secret society"—had essentially assigned themselves. Well, no matter...*)

"Leo recruited 35 women in Chicago by looking in the paper for people who'd just had a baby. We supplied the diapers and asked them to keep a diary of everything they did, because one of the things that really concerned us was this wasn't really a disposable diaper. It would last all night long, but it wasn't disposable. We had spent literally hundreds of hours at K-C trying to figure out how the hell we'd flush this thing down a toilet. We even had a glass toilet sitting up on a platform with pipes leading from it and we could see through it, see where it plugged."

Yeccchhhhh.

"But as it turned out," said Bill, "these women didn't have a problem disposing of the diaper. They threw it out with the garbage. They solved our problem."

"You mean you guys had never thought of throwing it in the garbage?" I asked, incredulously.

"We were fixated on it being flushable, because that's what the marketing people wanted—a flushable diaper," said Bill. "When we had sufficient data that this was a viable product, we presented this diaper to the marketing people. These guys were all very polite, sat there and listened. And finally, the executive VP said, 'You've done a very nice job but it's way too expensive and we couldn't sell anything like that.'

"Leo was so mad after that meeting he said 'Wilson, I'll work for you but I won't work for Kimberly-Clark.' I took the project, put it on the shelf, left it there."

""Bill was able to accept that reality—the idiocy of management," Leo chuckled mordantly.

"About a week or so later," said Bill, hardly missing a beat, "Leo went to these 35 women and said, 'We've got all the data we need so we aren't going to supply you with diapers.' And the women demanded more diapers. 'We don't care. Tell us how much it is, we'll pay for it, it's all right.'

"But we cut them off.

"Later I got a call from a lawyer in our legal department. He said, 'Bill, I've got the most peculiar letter here. It's from a lawyer in Chicago and I've looked him up and he's one of the top class-action guys in the country. Some women are bringing a case against us because we won't supply them with diapers. We don't make diapers, do we, Bill?'

"I said, 'I think I'd better come down and see you.'

"We decided that it would be cheaper to supply them with diapers than to fight a suit. So we went back and said, 'All right, we'll supply you with diapers. But if you have another kid I'm sorry—just one.'

"What better market research could you have? I took this up to marketing, but they still didn't think they could sell it.

"I found out later that the husband of one of the women on our test panel worked for Proctor and Gamble. So, the diary, the samples, the product got to P-and-G. Five years later, Pampers hit the street."

I thought the story ended there, a tale of the usual corporate paralysis. It was a story I had lived through more than once in a mature media industry that long ago had lost the romantic risk-impulse.

And I thought, for a moment, about how I and others in the business had taken psychic refuge in what might have been—if only someone had listened. It was, I realized, merely the moral arrogance of the defeated.

But now Bill and Leo added a new curlicue to their story: "The diaper got out because of a mistake that Kimberly made," Leo intoned. "Kimberly-Clark told Bill that he could sell whatever a hospital wanted to buy. This transformed the bureaucratic reality."

It was the Mobius strip of Bill's life: Kimberly-Clark shoveled "dog" businesses his way and Bill twisted them to realize the Tomahawk conspiracy's goal of starting the health-care business.

TRANSFORMING THE PASTURE.

One of Bill's "dog businesses," as it turned out, was the Kotex maternity pad.

"Now we had an entree, a legitimate reason for going into the health care market," said Bill. "When do women need the maternity pad? When they've had a baby. What did I have to go along with this? I pulled the diaper off the shelf, developed a diaper for newborns. We built a prototype machine in Memphis to make these things. And they were going like gangbusters.

"When Pampers hit the street, there was a guy over in the consumer division who had worked for me and he said to his boss, 'Wilson's got a diaper. He had it years ago. He's got a whole research program going on it. He's selling it in hospitals. And he's got a machine down in Memphis.' So the consumer division came and took it all."

"Just like *that*?" I asked. "What were your feelings?"

"You get pissed off a little bit," Bill shrugged. "But I

put it on the shelf in a nice package so that it could be taken off easily. I knew that some day we were gonna pull it off. I didn't realize that I would be the guy to do it. But how did I feel? I felt good. P-and-G was showing us how to sell it. We had a chance of being a good number-two."

Leo laughed. "No one who leads a corporation to the Promised Land can enter—it's the Moses story. The Bible says Moses got punished by God for not having faith. I don't think that was it. He dragged these poor people through the desert. They finally get to the Promised Land. Moses goes up into the mountain to get more guidance. They throw a wild party. He comes down and he's a party-pooper."

“That’s the classic problem,” I said. “The guy who starts something isn’t the one to run it into maturity.”

“You’re right,” said Bill. “If you’re going to use the maverick properly, you’ve got to convince ’em somehow to let go of it and go back and do it all over again.”

Lanny jumped in. “The maverick will get you to a whole new revenue stream. But once you find that stream, you’ll have to manage it with good operating managers who’ll build an organization around it. And all of that is antithetical to the maverick. The maverick is out looking for the next part of free range to tame.”

The word love is never
mentioned in big business.

Anita Roddick

7.
Love of Freedom.

MEASURING A MAVERICK'S EMOTIONAL IQ.

Bill took us to the airport and deposited us on the shuttle back to the West Coast and the real world, which was looking increasingly different, increasingly *un*real, as we explored the maverick way.

I was strangely reluctant to leave, although I knew we would be back to talk with Bill. I was developing a strange affection for the old guy, even though Bill still remained distant, elusive. He would happily share his stories and experiences—but, still, I had a sense that there were places he simply wouldn't allow us to go. And, of course, as a card-carrying journalist, those were the places that interested me the most.

As the chubby little 737 took off and climbed quickly above the desert city, Lanny began to rewind the day's conversation. I interrupted him with a question that had been nagging at me.

"People at Kimberly-Clark must have known that Bill was up to his maverick tricks. He must have had enemies."

"Some were," Lanny agreed. "It was the same old thing: he didn't acknowledge organizational boundaries. He knew where the fences were but he had a complete disregard for them.

"That's probably an overstatement. It's more correct to say that he was very aware of them, his organizational antennae were incredibly acute, but he recognized how permeable those boundaries actually were.

"But you have to remember that K-C made a heavy investment in Bill. Kimberly-Clark spent a lot of money on him. He had a foot in the in-crowd—he was part of the corporate apostolic succession—but he was also part of the fringe."

I didn't want to give up the point, perhaps for reasons that had to do more with my twisted history over the past half-decade, my current job as the official guru of the permanent newsroom revolution.

"Everyone has enemies in a corporate setting," I said. "How did Bill deal with the people who hated him?"

Lanny's reply startled me. "He honored them. He gave them time—he always gave anyone time, *anyone*. He never, never confronted them directly. And he never got angry. I think he knew that any time you get emotional you lose control and you give away too much. So from a very practical, pragmatic point of view too much passion was a disability. Bill learned that very early on, because that was hard-wired into Bill when I hooked up with him. Emotions, for him, got in the way.

"It's not that he's emotionless. He has a tremendously deep commitment to his kids, his wife—but while he brings incredibly intense passion to the job he doesn't demonstrate it. Because he realizes, and I think he's right, that if you get too demonstrative, you're not doing anybody any good. You're creating something that's counter-productive for yourself and everybody else. Bill's got this narrow emotional bandwidth in real life."

Lanny's comments made me squirm. No one would have accused me of narrow emotional bandwidth. In fact, I rather prided myself on what I called (*quite* privately) "the blowtorch." To me it was a tool for cutting through to a quick decision. After all, news deadlines were ruthlessly inflexible. You had to get things done—didn't you?

So, feeling a few hairs on the back of my neck prickling, I promptly changed the subject. And Lanny, perhaps sensing my unease, brought it straight back.

"I think Bill's very smart, but I don't think his IQ's in the genius category. What's more important is his emotional intelligence—it's real high. Bill would be a great golfer; he's really able to maintain his cool. I think he had this switch in his head—when something started to go differently than he expected, he'd switch into, 'Let's enjoy this, see where this goes.' Rather than, 'Oh, God, it can't go anywhere other than where I want it to go.' He didn't have a control problem. Which is really unusual. Most of us have a control problem..."

Ahhhh, yes, I thought. *We certainly do.*

"...but Bill doesn't seem to. He really doesn't."

I decided to take refuge in the journalist's final hideout, skepticism: "Bill always seems to say yes. Surely, Lanny, he must occasionally say no."

"His initial reaction was always yes. And then, later on he might kinda gravitate toward no," Lanny chuckled. "But he never said no immediately.

"I think Bill has the same urge to shoot down new ideas as we all do, but he's also savvy enough and emotionally controlled enough to be able to say, 'I'm not going to say that out loud. In fact, I'm going to say the exact opposite.' So, when he says yes, he's really saying, 'That's an *interesting* idea.'"

THE NARROW PATH BETWEEN FEAR AND LOVE.

"But I still haven't got a handle on what motivates him," I said, thinking back to Bill's impurturbability, his careful distancing that seemed tantalizing to the point of being infuriating.

"I think Bill is a compassionate Machiavelli," said Lanny. "He recognizes that ultimately the purpose of a task is to meet human needs. A lot of managers don't understand that. When push comes to shove, the needs of the organization supersede the needs of the individual. That's the stance of most managers, because they're afraid for their careers.

"I have a belief that the two primary emotions are fear and love and everything is interpolation between the two. The path that we're struggling to reveal here is love, whereas the other path is achievement-oriented. The maverick's path is truly based on self-denial. The other is looking at your career and where it's going. The maverick way is based on results, whereas the other path is interested in credit—who did it, blame or praise. The question that a Bill Wilson asks is, 'How does?' As opposed to what a lot of people ask, 'Who did?'

"In my experience the fear path is the dominant mode of behavior in organizations and love is not given a great deal of credibility. There's something very pure about Bill when what he does is motivated by love, selflessness; there's something tremendously liberating that frees the maverick, I think, to be a free range animal with confidence because they know they're ethical. It's clean. It's pure."

"There's a lot of power in knowing that you're right, but there's also a dark side to it," I objected. "Self-righteousness."

"I think the tool we're tweaking at is confidence," Lanny said. "And it's a genuine, pure kind of confidence that's based on being right without being righteous. It's a humble confidence. And that's not a technique. It's a character trait—you're born with it or it's born out of experience, or both. Bill had that. It allowed him to walk into the lion's den."

I recalled Jack Kimberly: "Sitting on a bridge tearing up hundred-dollar bills." My journalistic skepticism prompted me again: "I'm a little leery of this love-stuff."

"I was thinking about the classical Greek definitions of love," said Lanny. "Agape, selfless love. Philos, brotherly or sisterly love. And Eros, physical, sensual, esthetic love. What we're talking about is agape. So the maverick spirit is driven by giving."

"But a libertarian would say it's all a market relationship and you're getting something for this transaction," I said.

"There was a transaction going on with Bill," Lanny shrugged. "By operating this way, Bill was able to continue as a maverick. He bought freedom. But it wasn't just that he got 'freedom from...' It was also that he got 'freedom for.' He took freedom to the next level."

"Which is?"

"The freedom that a maverick loves is the freedom to love," Lanny replied. "It's loving the community of which they are a part. They love it so much that they are trying to renew it. They give themselves to it."

"Was love the glue that adhered people to Bill?" I asked.

"A shared value system," said Lanny. "A love of freedom. I think Bill recognized that in us before we recognized it in him and thus recognized it in ourselves. That may be unusual, but it's not complicated."

I glanced down, suddenly aware that we were over the vast, dun-colored collage of Los Angeles. As the plane descended through the tawny inversion layer, the city's distinctive, burnt-rubber odor flooded the cabin, an olfactory cue that I was home. Tucson seemed awfully far away, perhaps as far and as fictional as the Land of Oz. Had I seen the real wizard—or just a guy behind a curtain?

I returned to my workaday world, but after a few days, it began to seem, in subtle ways that eluded my immediate understanding, a trifle… well, *unreal.* It was as though I was photographing the reality around me—the hurly-burly of the newsroom and its feuds and triumphs and crises—through two lenses at the same time. One shooting from my point of view, as they say in Hollywood scripts; the other a wider shot, one in which I watched myself with a curious, almost scientific detachment. Much as Bill had been watching *me*.

This new life-movie that I was shooting was beginning to prompt me to look differently at the decisions that I was making, decisions that were my only real purpose in the *Register's* hive, since editors at my level certainly didn't cover the news or draw the maps or take the photos or do the research that actually appeared in print. Instead, we were… well, like officers on the great ship's bridge, issuing orders to the grease monkeys down in the engine room; correcting course around the reefs and pirate galleons.

But I couldn't be entirely sure about that role any

longer. Not when the question, "What would Bill do in this situation?" kept buzzing in my mind. Increasingly, alarmingly, I began to compare and contrast: Bill never seemed to issue orders, or even give much indication of where he wanted a conversation to go, but how were you supposed to get a newspaper published without telling people what to do?

Bill always said yes, but wasn't my role in the newsroom's deliberations to be the great nay-sayer? The guy with the needle looking for over-inflated balloons?

Bill, the sneak-thief, happily lying-stealing-cheating—was that any way to run a business based on trust? Hadn't I gotten my ass kicked more than once for the unforgivable sin of not keeping my betters sufficiently informed about what I was hatching back in my little empire of recipes and TV listings and movie critics?

And this stuff about "emotional IQ"—hell, I didn't want to touch that with a barge-pole. Nor did I really want to deal with Bill's amazing sense of patience: slogging away for a decade to put Kimberly-Clark into the health-care business. I hated waiting, sometimes (more often than I really cared to admit) paying a hell of a price for pushing too hard too soon. But you had to get things done before they could be done to you—right?

As Tucson's brief euphoria began to recede into the past, the book project began to slow. I began pecking away at the mass of interviews and written material, trying to shape it into something that would get Lanny and his, "Where's the book?" demands off my back.

As far as Lanny was concerned—and here we get into a strange psychological realm—whether anyone read the resulting book was a non-issue. He wanted it for Bill, as some kind of weird payoff. So why should I care?

But, in fact, I *did*. For reasons that I figured out only much, much later.

I didn't want to finish the book because I didn't want to be finished with Bill Wilson. Somehow, I knew, he was going to change things. No, not that: Somehow he was going to give me permission to change myself. Which, although I couldn't begin to imagine it at the time, is the only way it ever really works.

But that moment of enlightenment was months away, as amazing as it seems to write those words now. Instead, I went back to the sharpest, most destructive tool in my journalistic armamentarium—I began to probe Bill for weaknesses, places where I could trip him up, expose his secret something. After all, as I had learned in the journalist's graduate course in reality, something that's too good to be true usually is.

I decided to talk to others who had worked with and for him, a variant on the adage that no man is a hero to his valet. As usual, Bill thought that was a fine idea. And now that spring had returned to the Midwest, he suggested that I come out to the Ogdensburg farm, hole up there for a while, talk to Fred and Dick and other K-Cers, past and present. He'd give me carte blanche, wouldn't sit in on any of the sessions unless I allowed him, absolute freedom.

So, I put in for a week of vacation, booked a flight. I was ready to meet the Kimberly-Clark Mafia, Bill's "legitimate crazies."

When the leader's work
is done the people say,
'We did it ourselves!'

Lao-Tzu

8.
Running with a maverick's herd.

STRANGE CROPS ON THE FARM.

The drive up from Chicago took four hours. The interstate's grand sweep gave way to smaller highways, then meandering country roads passing Jeffersonian little towns with resonant names—Kaukana, Waupaca, Winnecone. Finally, Ogdensburg. A crossroads, really: stately white-steepled church on one corner, sleepy gas station on the other.

I followed Bill's instructions and, after missing his unmarked stub-road a couple of times, began the meandering drive up through a stand of somber pines that parted to reveal a rolling, sunny pasture. At the top of a rise sat what looked like a small village: houses, barns, various out-buildings. Quite a spread.

Bill waited for me at the end of the drive.

Our greeting was a bit shy—this would be our first time together without Lanny's intermediation (he was off globe-trotting for various clients). Bill led me inside, explaining proudly that Marg had designed the house. Its solid, hand-hewn timbers were pegged together, the interior redolent with a slightly musky, raw-wood perfume that brought back memories of my Iowa boyhood.

Marg once again set out Saran-wrapped sandwiches—pickle-pimento loaf, another cue for boyhood memories—then bustled quietly around the kitchen as Bill and I exchanged polite chit-chat.

He offered a quick tour of the farm and I eagerly accepted.

Collecting—the basement was jammed with a seemingly chaotic profusion of this-and-that: a cluttered gem and minerals shop, drawers bulging with rocks of every size, shape, provenance; a wall lined with antique hand tools, well-worn, labor-stained; then a massive collection of tin soldiers, whole armies in tidy drawers and antique boxes: Boers, Grenadiers, Zouaves, Musketeers.

Bill opened a door, snapped on a hanging overhead bulb that revealed shelves groaning with notebooks, files, archival boxes. Damn near every piece of paper he had ever touched in his 40-odd years at Kimberly-Clark. Plus racks of audio and videotapes—meeting after meeting that he had recorded during the years under Bill Gordon's tutelage, meetings that helped to create the scientific backbone for what became Synectics.

"One of these days I'll have to index all this stuff," said Bill with an exasperated wave of his hand.

We climbed back upstairs, emerged back into the sunny summer day. Bill explained that he had "collected" the farm itself, starting up by the road with the first 90 acres in 1958, living for a while in the old yellow homestead I had passed on the way in. Then he had added this piece and that as neighbors retired or died.

His empire now included fields, forests, even a bona fide swamp I got a sense that Bill was a guy who liked a certain distance between himself and the neighbors. It reminded me of his curious diffidence; his ability to listen without displaying the slightest hint of what he was thinking.

We passed a field of ancient, horse-drawn field implements rusting quietly in the tall grass and arrived at a big, windowless metal building. Bill pulled back a wall-sized sliding door revealing a phalanx of old farm tractors, each in perfect running order, 32 in all. Tucked away in a corner was a vintage fire engine, once one of Ogdensburg's finest. In other buildings were old horse-drawn sleighs, Conestoga wagons, buckboards in various stages of restoration—Bill, the one-man historical society. Some of the artifacts were mere fragments, bare remainders of their former function, a wagon tongue here, a scattering of wheel spokes there. *Waiting*, just as Bill seemed to wait, endlessly patient, for things to fall together, just so.

We wandered on, came to a curious A-frame structure. It looked like a steeple after the church had dematerialized beneath it. Bill laughed and explained that he had brought a bunch of O-C Group fellows out one weekend to do some brainstorming. Their challenge had been to design an innovative outhouse—they had certainly succeeded.

It was all mind-boggling. "Collecting" hardly began

to describe what I had just seen. Gems, tin soldiers, swords, guns, toy trains, tractors—what was the thread that knit them together?

Then, with a sudden jolt, I recalled one of the lynchpins of Synectics: the notion that you could generate seemingly irrelevant material (say, ideas about rocks when you were working on a problem about computer software), then "force-fit" these two wildly different images to produce a stunning *aha!* And now, I had the curious feeling that I was dipping my toes in the headwaters of the river that had brought that idea, that technique, down through the years. To the curious crew at Synectics. To Lanny. To me.

We drove down to yet another farmhouse tucked back into the pines (planted years before by Bill and his kids). The house would be my base of operations as, one by one, members of Wilson's secret society drove the 60 or so miles over from Neenah.

As I waited, I flipped back through the old Rose Moss book. A passage caught my eye: "Bill's office is like his basement, a map of his mind. It divides almost equally into areas of fine-grain, systematic order showing access to large fields of explored and generally agreed-upon knowledge; and to smaller areas of factual information; and also to other areas where new materials like reports, letters and articles become heaps."

TAMING A 'BULL IN THE WOODS.'

"Fred Hrubecky," said my first visitor, pumping my hand, moving into the room as though he owned it.

I knew a few things about Fred. He and Bill had worked shoulder-to-shoulder for years. It was Hrubecky, the engineering genius, who toiled to perfect the "diaper that worked"; Hrubecky, the engineering eccentric, who constructed the infamous "glass toilet" in an attempt to satisfy the marketing department's obsession with the diaper's "flushability"; Fred, the unorthodox researcher, whose newborn served as a test-subject for the leaky diaper prototypes.

And it was Fred, not Bill, who had quit when the diaper was squelched.

Fred got right down to business, hardly pausing to scoop up a handful of cookies that Marg had thoughtfully baked and which had magically appeared on a plate in the farmhouse kitchen. He punctuated his rapid-fire monologue with explosions of laughter, each marking some moment of supreme corporate insanity, or one of the Wilson Mafia's merry pranks.

But, as he talked, I noted that Fred and Bill differed in one key aspect: Whereas Bill told his stories with a kind of detached objectivity, much as a scientist might describe something interesting in a test tube, Fred's were fierce moral tales, full of villainous villains and injured heroes (in many cases, Fred himself). Such as: "I remember the first time that I wrote a memo saying that disposable diapers could be a two-hundred million dollar business. That's when they (management) were all convinced that I was a stupid goddamn immature bohunk who didn't know his ass from page two," the tirade punctuated by laughter. "Now it's more like $4 *billion*."

Fred's stories gradually put something he said about Bill into a different perspective: "Wilson avoided a lot more pain than I did because Bill's not abrasive. Always been a gentleman. He's always been a pathfinder kind of a guy. Whereas I'm more of a bull in the woods—a bowl 'em over, knock 'em down kind of a guy. Bill was able to maneuver around people and do what he wanted to do. I would simply do what I wanted to do and then say, 'OK, what you gonna do about it?' High stakes kind of stuff.

"I was collected as a maverick," he laughed. "It was one reason I stayed on for 26 years. It was that good start with Bill's group where I got to see the big picture—the opportunity picture—without being completely turned off by the company's uptight culture."

Fred was initially enlisted in the conspiracy to run Convertors, the company that Wilson, without so much as a nod to upper management, created to produce hospital operating room "packs" from the new-fangled nonwovens that were beginning to flow into the product pipeline.

"My first day on the job, I showed up in a white shirt and tie," said Fred. "Then we went down to the Diamond Match building in Oshkosh and unloaded a truckload full of Kaycel. I loved it immediately! That was the last time I wore a tie for a long time.

"The group was quite loose," he laughed again. "It was also very hush-hush, and with good reason. The research atmosphere at that time was incredibly stuffy and rigid and puritan in the worst kind of way. And the Operational Creativity Group (*Wilson's previous assignment*) had generated all kinds of animus based on the privileges they had and that other people did *not* have."

"So there are some clear advantages to being underground?" I asked.

"Without a doubt. That's something Bill practiced to an art, and all of us learned eventually. There are times when you do the 'Hey lookame!' Because you don't have a big political downside. But there are a lot more other times when you," another manic laugh, "go underground and pop up somewhere else."

But, of course, there's a downside in the maverick's fondness for secrecy. Fred readily agreed.

"I think you'll find very few people in Kimberly-Clark who understand how much Bill contributed. Because we were looked on with ridicule. And laughter. The thing that always amazed me, though, was how easy it was for them to forget the source of the successes."

Fred took another nibble of Marg's cookie, his brow furrowed. "I've never had a line on whether I would have done better at Kimberly-Clark if I had had Bill's accepting attitude—or maybe I'd have done worse if I hadn't been a maverick and made things happen in spite of the roadblocks. I've seen it happen both ways.

"I have no regrets about my career at Kimberly-Clark. The only time I really questioned working there was during a product recall. I was fighting hard for it and the guy I was working for was saying no. I was formulating my letter of resignation.

"It was a good lesson for me, though. There had been times when I was critical of people who hadn't stood up, and I didn't stand up immediately, either."

"What would Bill have done in your shoes?" I asked.

"I don't think Wilson would have done anything different, with one exception. He would never even *think* about a letter of resignation." No laugh this time. Fred looked a little grim. He thought for a moment, then added: "He probably would have done one other thing more effectively—because of his better personal insight into people. Somehow or other, Wilson would have gotten inside that guy's head and convinced him that it was in his best career interests to do the right thing for the customer. I was unable to do that."

"Did you share your problem with Bill at the time?"

Fred shifted, a little nervously.

"No. He was in Europe."

"Still," I said, "there's a trans-Atlantic phone."

"That's true," said Fred. "I guess at that time..." and then he lapsed into an uncomfortable silence.

"What happened to Bill over there?" I persisted.

Fred's answer was oblique: "If you think we're rigid, the Europeans are a hell of a lot more rigid. And Bill had a low regard for a lot of that rigidity."

"Was Europe a stumble?" I asked.

"His career took a downward trend after that European thing," said Fred after a long pause. "That's when they brought him back and made him head of Energy. It was a real backwater.

"The company's view was, 'We're not in the energy business, we're in the customer-product business.' Which is typical in any industry: the stuff that doesn't get in the final container is trivial and unimportant. Although the consequences of failure can be just as bad as a lousy product.

"So, I think it was universally considered that Bill had been really slapped hard. He got stuck in an office out in the boonies. He had a couple of guys working for him who were white-socks-type guys that are easy to scoff at, particularly if you're stupid and ignorant and don't understand what they're talking about, which qualifies most people."

I was about to dig into this new insight—could it be

that Bill's maverick ways had finally brought him up lame?—but then another car pulled up in the drive.

We had another guest.

HOW TO STEAL A PARTY.

It was Dick Loescher, another Kimberly-Clark retiree and one of Bill's key allies for more than four decades at the company. Loescher had worked for Bill, with Bill, and at some remove from him, but always cherry-picking opportunities or maverick-candidates for his friend to develop. That's what he had done in dispatching young Lanny Vincent to present his resume to Wilson back in the early '80s.

It was also clear, from our prior discussions, that Bill deeply admired Dick, describing him as a Renaissance man plunked down in modern-day Wisconsin. Since leaving the company, Dick had reinvented himself as a student, artist (his whimsical wire sculptures dotted Bill's barn-cum-house walls) and a published poet. He had led troops of Sea Scouts, served on this board and that, taught college courses, done the usual post-retirement consulting gigs.

The man who tromped up the stairs was a big fellow, Jackie Gleason-big, moving with a big man's delicate, dancelike grace. He wore a jaunty Greek fisherman's cap perched atop his massive, white-fringed head. He laughed easily, but a little warily. After all, I was the dude from La-La Land, and he wasn't sure what I was about to do to his longtime associate, mentor and friend.

Soon, he and "Freddie," as he called Hrubecky, fell into happy reminiscences about their years with Wilson, the battles they had fought, even the occasional defeats they had suffered at the hands of corporate opponents—the ones Fred sneeringly called, "*rigid*."

"It was B-S that we really knew what we were doing," said Fred of the Operational Creativity Group and its successor, New Products. "All of us knew that we didn't really know, but we knew that we were participating in a happening. If we were asked, 'What're you doing in New Products?' we could give specifics, but we knew everything could change tomorrow."

Added Dick, "That was one of our key lying techniques. We could give reports, right?"

Fred giggled at the recollection. "Oh, *yeah…*"

"…and we were lying through our teeth! Bill would shape it a little bit, package it for upward consumption."

"The B-S was primarily external. It was survival B-S," Fred added.

"And we had to support our cover," said Dick. "You had to do this stuff somewhere within the framework of what the company was willing to provide.

"Allow me to illustrate what I mean about cheating and stealing," he continued. "Bill had a retirement party, and in the room were twenty or thirty people. All hand-picked by Bil, at one time or another during their careers. I looked around the room and asked, 'Hey, how many of you people paid to go to this party?' Answer to that—nobody. 'How many of you have gone to a Kimberly-Clark-sponsored retirement party where they paid for everything?' Same answer—nobody. 'Well, then, would some of you explain how this thing works?' I would pick on somebody like Freddie and he would, *wham!* come right through with some plausible theory. Everyone had an instant answer and every one was different."

After our laughter subsided, I asked how Bill had assembled his teams of corporate misfits and rebels and kept them from imploding? How did he put those teams together in the first place?

Dick and Fred glanced at one another and grinned.

You had to demonstrate that you were non-conventional to be included," said Fred.

"We used to have ways of picking up symptoms," said Dick. "You look for diversity in the person's background. Say you interview a guy like Fred—here he is, his college grade point sucks, there are a lot of negative things on paper...*hmmmm.* But, after talking, it comes through that this guy is different in ways that could be useful because he's not afraid of failure, he's got initiative, he's creative, he's got a lot of stuff that comes out if you listen during an interview."

"Another good way to find out about people," said Fred, "is by asking, who are their enemies? I'll think, 'There's gotta be something here because someone who's a complete asshole hates this person, so therefore he's got to have something really promising if he challenges this really staid, formal, rigid, restricted person.' That means he's flexible, stretches things, looks at things differently. The enemy list is important."

And if you weren't on an enemies list before you joined Wilson's circle, you sure were afterwards, said Fred. "One manager had a meeting with his people and he pointed to me and said, 'I don't want you guys to be anything like that fellow.' The best compliment I'd ever had."

I quizzed Dick about Bill's time in Europe back in the mid-'70s. Dick ducked it with the excuse that he had been out of touch with Bill, up to his eyeballs with Purchasing issues, cleaning out the deadwood—a crock! Dick and Fred's reluctance to discuss it was catnip for the journalistic kitty. I finally had my gotcha!

PUTTING 'ALWAYS SAY YES' TO THE ULTIMATE TEST.

After they left, I returned to the Rose Moss book. She had, it seemed to me, skipped rather lightly through what was obviously a real career moo-pie: "Europe would prove a difficult assignment for Wilson. He went without the support of the network of people he had established at Neenah and in the United States. He had none of his old mentors and protectors by him. He was dealing with people and cultures new to him. Many of their assumptions would fly in the face of his own.

"In Europe it was difficult for Wilson to assess his margins of safety correctly, to know what risks it would be safe to take in personal relations, in customs or in the legal systems. It was difficult for him to know accurately where he could circumvent conventional procedures without getting into trouble—and his experience in Neenah had strengthened the tendency to circumvent already visible in his college days. He was alone in unknown territory."

So, after dinner, I cranked up the Wilson story machine. Bill told me about his adventures in running Kimberly-Clark's troubled European operation, how he had consolidated divisions, attacked waste, done deals in the strange culture in which he found himself. Things moved at a different pace over there; everything had its own strange etiquette. These were people who decided who and what you were by the way you delivered an after-dinner toast.

I asked if he had had mavericks in his operation. Yes, he said, he had a particular memory of a foreman in an English paper-mill. "He went from division to division doing almost the same damn thing that I was doing. He cut the waste in that mill from about ten or twelve percent to under one."

"How did you protect that maverick?" I asked.

Bill grinned. "I changed the mill manager. I put someone in there who wouldn't be looking over the maverick's shoulder all the time, interfering with him. Let the maverick run on the free range."

As he talked, it reinforced my impression that these had been Bill's toughest years. He traveled constantly, but far from the typical executive's imperial progress through the provinces, Bill would drop in at plants a day early, unaccompanied, would wander among the big machines talking to the men and women on the line. By the time the mill executives found out he was there, Bill would have a pretty good picture of what was working and wasn't. It was straight out of his earliest Kimberly-Clark experiences when Bill's boss asked him to "find out about wood" at the Spruce Falls mill.

Bill showed me a watercolor that Marg had painted of their house near Oxford, England, a fairy-tale, thatched-roof Elizabethan cottage. He hadn't been able to spend much time in that house, he muttered as I enthused over it. In fact, he felt a little guilty because his peripatetic life left Marg to cope with the kids, including a son who had been diagnosed as dyslexic. And, as the Moss book made clear, it was also a time when the numbers, for the first time, weren't breaking in Bill's favor: "In Neenah, the series of reorganizations begun under Guy Minard (*Kimberly-Clark CEO from 1968-1971*) speeded up under Darwin Smith (*CEO, 1971-1992*). The pressure was on to produce profits. Wilson began well. Foreign consumer and service products registered a 20% revenue gain. But changes raised costs and operating margins contracted from 11% in 1974 to 7.9% in 1975, confirming Neenah's vision of Wilson as a big spender sloppy about costs."

And then he got wind that a younger executive was slotted for Europe. Bill had initiated a ten-year plan for turning around the European operation, but the turnaround didn't come in time. Moss, again: "This was no climate to favor Wilson's eagerness for fundamental change and the desire to introduce the new in ways that take long-term vision and time.... Wilson had contributed to a turnaround, but it was a sensitive assignment and much of it went against the grain."

Which brought us to The Question. Bill must have seen it coming, for he answered it without my asking.

"I got pulled out," he said. "And what were they going to do with me? They stuck me into Energy and Environment. And everybody I saw, particularly my old people, were all— 'Gee, Bill, a real comedown for you.'"

But Bill's earlier work on trends had primed him to look at environmental concerns in a very different way than most corporate bulls of the era saw them: not as nagging irritations but as ripe opportunities.

"I said, 'I don't know anything about energy and environment. It's a great place to find out what's going on.'"

In fact, environment was a classic free range—a place to explore and return with exotic new "products," such as the evil waste that the company was paying $550 per 55-gallon drum for disposal. Bill found another company that wanted to *buy* the gunk for $700 per drum.

"I'll never forget the first day I sat down with these two guys," said Bill, recalling his entire staff at the time. "They were having a problem over at the Lakeview Mill in the wastewater treatment plant. It was plugging up with a kind of fungus.

"I said, 'Why don't you toss a few brown trout in there?'

"They said, 'Why would you do that, Bill?'

"I told them, 'We had the same problem in Germany and we threw a bunch of brown trout fingerlings in there and in no time it was clean as a whistle. Every once in a while the guys would fish 'em out for their dinner. When Darwin Smith came over we served him trout for dinner.'

"These guys said, 'Jeez, Bill, we aren't trying to make a business out of this. We don't want a fish farm.'

"And I said, 'Fellas, I'm a businessman. I want to try anything that will save us money or earn us money. So you get some fingerlings and stick 'em in that tank and see what happens.'

"When I left that job five years later, we were saving

over $80 million a year. And that went straight to the bottom line. I couldn't have generated $80-million in profit in Europe in ten years. They aren't doing it yet. So what if everybody felt I was demoted. I never felt that way. It was a challenge. I didn't know a damned thing about it. But I set out to figure out how to save as much energy for the corporation as I could."

It was, I observed, the essence of Bill's motto: Always Say Yes. Which triggered another tale—this one about yes taken to its greatest extreme.

"Leroy Peterson was in charge of all of Kimberly-Clark's manufacturing, engineering and research. I didn't work for him, but he called me in one day and said, 'I was in a meeting today and there were thirty people there. There's something wrong if I have to have that many people there. Can you help me think through what I should be doing?'

"I got his organization charts. I cleared off the dining room table and I started juggling the pieces, trying to fit them together. I wasn't getting anywhere. His organization was a jungle.

"So, I got a clean sheet of paper, put Peterson up at the top of the page and asked myself, What's he responsible for? For the mills, for engineering, for research.

"I looked at the different parts of engineering—there's electrical, steam, civil part, mechanical part. Then I thought, Over here in engineering is steam. Over here in research is water—you can't have steam without water. Over here, not in Peterson's organization, is Bill Wilson in energy and environment and he's involved in steam and water, trying to use it more efficiently, clean it up. So, it was obvious that all these bits and pieces ought to go together.

"I took about 95 percent of my job and fit it into Peterson's organization. I had kept my boss informed that I was doing this project. The only thing he said was, 'Jeez, Bill, you've done yourself out of a job. What are you going to do?'

"I said, 'It doesn't make any difference to me what I do. If Kimberly can't find a job for me, I can find a job. Doesn't bother me in the least.'"

Which, when I thought about it, was a corollary of Always Saying Yes.

Bill presented the plan. Peterson accepted enthusiastically, then walked it through Kimberly-Clark's executive suite.

"I went over for a meeting with Leroy and he said, 'Well, Bill, I've gotten permission to push the button.'

"Then he said, 'I want you to come over and work for me.'

"I said, 'Fine. What do you want me to do?'

"He said, 'I want you to do what you do best.'

"I said, 'I'll do that—but I know what I do best. You don't have to tell me.' And, he didn't, either...."

Thus did Bill become vice president for Exploratory Projects. He had a title, an office and not much else—no staff, no mission statement no clear marching orders.

"Were you nervous about that?" I asked.

"About *what*?"

"Taking on that job?"

"Hell, no," he replied, as if I had asked him if the world was a cube. "That was an ideal job to have. I could go anywhere, do anything, muck around any place I wanted to."

"But there's a downside, potentially," I said, hoping that Bill wouldn't intuit that I was asking the question both of him, and myself, as my brain flooded with memories of my exotic "Synectics Guy" job, the one I had tried so hard to shuck.

"What's the downside?" Bill asked.

"The downside is that you're just sort of floating out there. That sort of job would make a lot of people crazy."

For example, I thought sourly, *me*. And when I had finally been "promoted" out of that position, I had left it with a sense of relief, leavened with a nagging feeling that, somehow, I had failed. No, that wasn't it, of course: The job had failed me. I had a laundry-list of reasons: newsroom resistance to change, a flawed reorganization, politic—the usual villians.

Bill, of course, disagreed: "You've got time to think. You can wander around and see what's going on and get to know a lot of people you don't know very well, possibly help them."

His remark reminded me that I had actually *liked* that part of the job. In the end I had created a sort of unofficial network, people I visited every day or so, sources of wonderful news and gossip. Could I help it, I wondered, if no one else in the newsroom was particularly interested in what I was discovering on my perambulations? Or, perhaps, I hadn't known what to *do* with the nuggets I was picking up, out there on what I now realized was the free range.

"If you put a certain kind of person in that job they would be very nervous because they don't have any power," I said. Exactly! And yet, I had found the lack of any "real" power, in the end, strangely liberating, for reasons that I had been unable to articulate.

"The hell they don't have power," Bill scoffed. "They just need to know how to *use* it." His grin indicated that he had never had any doubts about *that*.

And that, of course, led to an inescapable regret:

If only I had known Bill Wilson a decade ago..

I spent a restless night in the little farmhouse, replaying my encounter with Wilson and all of the second thoughts and regrets that it had prompted.

I recalled the early '90s, the Great Newsroom Reorganization, when I had been scooped up into an altogether strange job in a revolution, deep down, that I hated. And yet, like every card-carrying journalist, I had an agenda, usually expressed over beer and resentments, for changing the profession, making it better, more… perfect. And, of course, *they* were always standing in the way of the newspaper realizing its true potential.

Now the thought nagged: I had been given an extraordinary amount of freedom. Maybe not intentionally. But that was the net effect of the job I had been given. *Freedom.*

To change things.

So, why hadn't I changed anything?

What would Bill have done in my place? It was a question that I had been asking myself with unnerving frequency. Why didn't I ask Bill? Perhaps because he would have offered yet another obscure story and left me to fish for the moral.

In time, I would have caught it.

And then, I would have to do something different, a prospect that was too scary to contemplate.

Dick Loescher had called working with Bill like walking on a "slippery slope." How true!

The study of organization has rested on one assumption: that there is or must be a single 'right' form of organization... It has become clear that organization is not an absolute. It is a tool for making people productive in working together.

Peter S. Drucker

9.
THE MAVERICK MANAGER.

LETTING THE BEAR INTO THE CABIN.

The next visitor, John Raley, 48, was considerably younger than Bill and had the virtue of working currently for Kimberly-Clark, where he was the manager of Intellectual Property. He had, I knew from Lanny's briefing, compiled an enviable record at K-C, starting in 1982 in diaper R&D; then joining Bill's Innovation Management Group in 1984. Four years later, he went to the International Group to support existing oversees businesses and start new ones. In 1997, Raley was asked by the company to write a manual on how to launch new businesses.

Shortly before I left for Wisconsin, John had sent me an e-mail that piqued my interest:

"When I first met Bill Wilson, I asked someone (I seem to remember it was Lanny) what it was like to work for Bill. The answer I received was: It was like going bear hunting with Bill. You and Bill and the others arrive at a hunting cabin in the evening and turn in for a good night's sleep. The next morning, you awake and find that Bill is gone.

"A quick search confirms that Bill is missing. About that time, you hear Bill's shouts coming from the woods. 'Open the door. Open the door!'

"Looking outside, you see Bill running down the path with a bear in hot pursuit. If Bill has to slow down to open the door to the cabin, the bear will surely catch him.

So, you open the door and yell for Bill to run faster. Just as he gets to the door, the bear nipping at his heels, he quickly steps aside. The bear, unable to stop, hurtles into the cabin.

"Bill quickly slams the door and heads back up the trail, yelling, 'You take care of that one. I'll go get another.' That's what it's like to work for Bill."

Then he had appended this tantalizing postscript:

"Is 'Maverick' a noun, adjective, verb, or state of mind? If you truly understand, the answer is YES."

Now he sat opposite me at the kitchen table, looking every inch the brainy ascetic, eyes glittering behind thick specs. He punctuated his remarks with frequent paroxysms of laughter, prompting me to observe that these K-C'ers laughed a *lot*.

"What did you learn about managing, particularly managing mavericks, from Bill?" I asked.

"Bill views people as assets, not as factors of production," said John. "In spite of everything you read in the literature—'Our employees are our most valuable asset'—it's bull. Almost every organization operates by authorized head-count. Now that I've got these slots, I go find warm bodies to fill them. That's no different than building a warehouse and filling its empty shelves. Factors of production. The way Bill ran his shop, the deal he had with management was—he didn't want any authorized slots. Because the organization forces you to fill 'em or lose 'em. Bill's deal was, 'When I find someone I want, I want the slot.' That's viewing the human being as an asset."

EVALUATING PERFORMANCE WITHOUT NORMS.

"Once he had his assets," I asked, feeling a little skeptical, "how did he evaluate them?"

"I don't think you can in the classic sense," said John. "Because evaluations tend to be structured, measured against norms, measured against expectations. But a maverick has no norms and the only expectation is that he's bringing back something different. If it's different you can't measure it. So, you have to look for surrogates—how many people are finding value in what he's bringing back."

"In a way," I responded, "to protect a maverick you have to *become* a maverick. When Human Resources comes around with an evaluation form, as the maverick's protector you've got to be willing to say it doesn't work."

"I worked for Bill from '84 to '88 and never had a performance review," John responded. "I once asked Bill about that. He said, 'Do you *need* one?'"

John shook with laughter at the recollection. "I said, 'Well, I just thought we had to do these things.'

"Bill's answer was, 'If you think you're doing a good job and I think you're doing a good job, isn't that all we need?'

"On many occasions Bill has said that you don't manage for performance by providing annual course-corrections. Bill's definition of managing for performance is frequent course corrections, in the sense of adjusting the steerage just a touch."

"How did Bill adjust your steerage?"

"Bill seldom offered an opinion. If he *did*, you were in deep trouble. Bill would tend to interview you: 'What have you done today?' That's a hell of a course-correction question. If you haven't done anything that you think is valuable, I guarantee you, tomorrow you're going to work harder. Because you don't want to say, *Nuthin*'.

"He'd ask questions: 'What happened?' 'Why did it happen that way?' 'What do you think would happen if?' That's how Bill would do course-corrections."

REFUSING TO GIVE AN ORDER.

"What if you went to Bill," I asked, "and you said, 'I don't know what to do. What should I do?' It's the classic offload question that managers get all the time—which most managers, deep down, love to get."

"Bill would take a couple minutes to think about it. He wasn't thinking about the answer; he was thinking about possible answers: 'You could do this. Or you could do that. This is another possibility. What do you think about these?' There was a lot of wisdom in that approach—Bill was teaching, 'It's OK to brainstorm and then go back and evaluate the options.' Bill was providing options. Then he would help you sort them.

"By doing this, he was developing your ability to think these things through. By not providing the answer, he avoided taking any ownership. He offered options because he didn't want to take away from your ownership or your freedom.

"In hindsight," John continued, "I apply that to my current leadership positions. I'll seldom tell my people what to do. I'll purposely throw out three or four options; some I don't believe in myself. But whether I believe in them isn't the point. Because, if I make a decision, then I own it."

"But what if somebody makes a selection from your options and it's obvious that it's not the right thing to do?" I asked.

"If it's an immediate selection, I might say, 'Let's look at these other things and see if we can improve on the idea.' But, if the person picks one that you think is a non-starter, you're faced with a very interesting decision. It's called risk-management and the freedom of trust. Bill would let you go. Sometimes you discovered the brick wall right in front of your nose. But that's part of learning."

"This prompts the compensation question," I said. "How do you pay a maverick?"

"Most organizations pay an individual one dime more than they would take (from another employer). Bill recognized that the cost of the employee is a very small percentage of the overall scheme. Bill could increase my salary fifteen percent and in the grand scheme of things it wouldn't affect anything. On average in the US, labor is fifteen percent of the cost of manufactured goods. OK, so you increase that by ten percent—it's now sixteen and a half percent. Big deal.

"Organizations have boundary conditions, salary controls and stuff like that. Bill did as much as he could within these constraints, but a big part of his compensation was freedom."

"Money doesn't motivate you in the same way?" I asked.

"I view money as paying me for what I did. I view freedom as paying me for what I'm going to do. So, money to me is past-tense and I don't really care that much, because mavericks are future-tense.

"You've heard Bill say that he doesn't own a computer and he would barely know how to turn one on. But any time I went to Bill with a computer request, his answer was, 'Where do I sign?' He had no idea what I was buying. But that was part of my compensation. Freedom to do these things has value.

"Here's another example: In the mid-'80s, Darwin Smith (*then Kimberly-Clark's CEO*) said, 'You can have any personal computer you want as long as it has IBM on it.' Bill bought me a Macintosh, because that's what I wanted to run an application that hadn't been written for the IBM operating system. As far as I know, I'm the only person in K-C who got a Mac.

"But that was Bill investing in his people. To me, Bill was saying, 'I know you're going to do something wonderful with this.' That gives me something to live up to. I'll stay up nights not to let Bill down. So, that Mac is a cheap investment. Bill has told me many times that investing in people is the cheapest investment an organization can make. And that goes back to the question: Do you view people as assets or as factors of production."

APPRECIATING THE ART OF LETTING-GO.

Raley, in looking back at his career, post-Wilson, now realized that Bill had subtly encouraged him—cut the fence—so that he could make frequent forays into the free range. All well and good, but what about when the maverick returns?

John's answer seemed, initially, off-the-mark. (But then, I quickly reminded myself, that's a maverick trait.)

"Mavericks tend to get dinged by organizations because they don't want to *own* something. Mavericks like to find something, bring it back to the pasture, let go of it, then go back out to the free range. Mavericks don't want to stay in the pasture and manage what they've brought back. Because that would mean they're no longer a maverick.

"The downside to that is that mavericks must have a martyr complex. Mavericks have to be OK with the fact that organizations are not going to reward them for bringing something new back to the pasture. Organizations are going to reward the person who took it and grew it."

"Leo Shapiro called Wilson a 'Moses', because he got to the river but couldn't get across to the promised land."

"Correct," said John. "I'll put that into my own context. My technician and I hand-made the first Huggies with super-absorbent in them and gave them to moms and then got the project started.

"The project was then handed off to an execution group. I never even got a thank you. But I'm OK with that. A lot of people wouldn't."

"Go back to the point at which you handed off your development," I asked. "What was going on at that point?"

"I knew it worked. I could envision the future. For me the thrill of discovery was over. I'd made a hundred of these things. I didn't want to make a hundred more. I wanted to go back out and find something new.

"One of the things I learned from Bill is that when mavericks do this, management needs to recognize and appreciate it.

"After all, the art of management is matching the right skills with the right needs."

THE VIRTUES OF INEQUALITY.

This argued, said John, for managing mavericks *differently*, applying different evaluation criteria to their efforts, compensating them differently, all things that were politically incorrect.

John grinned in agreement. "I'd never looked favorably on compartmentalizing people—in a nice way—until I was around Bill."

"That goes to an issue of the top-level manager who gets hinky when he gets a sense that you're managing people differently," I said, speaking from first-hand knowledge. Back in my earliest days at the *Register*, when the paper had a richly-deserved reputation for being a Southern California nut-case, many of my first hires were folks who lacked—shall we say?—a proper pedigree. But as I hired them, collected them, I now realized, they had a way of doing strange, off-the-wall things and writing wonderful, wacky stories. Pretty soon we were up there with *real* newspapers, elbowing them aside for awards.

But as the paper "improved," it got harder to properly defend my oddballs and misfits, such as the writer (now a best-selling author) who told me he was feeling a little tired and would be leaving for a few days, long before he had accrued a single day of vacation.

"We have no stars here!" the editor thundered, prompted by the whines of staffers who thought I was showing "favoritism," or some such corporate sin. But, I thought, wasn't that the point? To create stars. Nurture them, encourage them, use them?

"Mavericks have to be treated differently," said John. "I strongly believe that people should not be treated the same. It's like in football. Everybody on the team is playing the same game with the same goal, but the expectations for the quarterback are different than the expectations for the fullback. And that's OK."

"How explicit do you have to be about that in terms of the rest of the organization?" I asked.

"I think it's got to be organic, in the sense that you might identify some people, pull them off to the side. You wouldn't make it high visibility, no announcements on the bulletin board, because mavericks don't like to be targets."

THE ART OF LOOKING THE OTHER WAY.

"So, if I'm hearing you correctly," I said, "mavericks must be managed with a pretty light hand."

"Let me give you an example," said John. "I'm active in the Masons. Back in '94, I was the leader of the

Masonic lodges in Appleton. People were moaning about how the organization was stale, wasn't going anywhere.

"So, I started all sorts of activities by encouraging others to get something going. During this period of time, I'd say I didn't know about two-thirds of the activities until they were already organized. Now, for a command-and-control freak, that would just rip you apart. I thought it was wonderful! Look at this stuff that's going on—and I don't have to do anything!

"Under the Masonic rules you have to ask the state head for permission to violate a given regulation. I broke so many that finally the state head called me and said, 'Look, why don't you just write me a letter once a quar-

ter telling me what rules you broke and I'll say OK and that way we've taken care of the paperwork part.'"

"Pretty good way to protect a maverick," I laughed. "Just 'fess up once in a while."

"If a maverick has to come and ask, 'Mother, may I,' every time he wants to break a rule, there's going to be a fair share of dismay. But if the maverick checks in quarterly, 'Here are the ten rules I broke and two of 'em didn't work out so good,' you're a winner."

THE MAVERICK PARADOX.

I was interested in the current population of mavericks at Kimberly-Clark as a way to probe Bill's legacy.

"I don't think there are as many mavericks as there were in Bill's day," said John. "Organizations tend to go through cycles where mavericks are more or less visible. Right now, K-C is going through a cycle where mavericks would prefer to have a lower profile. That's not good or bad—just the way it is."

But, he added, the relative lack of mavericks posed an interesting paradox. "You would think that the bigger an organization, the more it can afford mavericks. If you assume that a group of mavericks costs you a certain amount every year, the bigger an organization, the smaller that amount in percentage terms. It becomes a rounding error. So, why not have it?

"The paradox is that a large organization's primary function is to maintain the status quo. A small organization might be eighty percent administration, twenty percent mavericks. As that organization grows, that maverick group is staying constant and diminishing in percentage terms. So, eventually it's 99-to-one. That's why I think a central question is: How to protect the maverick in the large organization? For an answer to that, you should refer to Bill's life cycles of a business, because the nature of protection in each stage is very, very different."

I made a mental note to pursue that line when Bill and I talked. But meanwhile I had one last, nagging question.

"From the day that I encountered Wilson until now, this guy has in some way influenced me to think about making some risky moves in my own life. And I'm damned if I know how he *did* it."

John laughed. "And Bill will continue to have an influence over your life, like it or not. Because, what Bill has done is put your imagination into play about what could be. And his story-telling has sanctioned dreams. Bill activated my subconscious. And by doing that, things came up to the conscious level."

The question, left unstated: Did I really want that to happen..?

An organization is a system with a logic of its own and all the weight of tradition and inertia. The deck is stacked in favor of the tried and proven way of doing things and against the taking of risk and striking out in new directions.

John D. Rockefeller III

10. MAVERICKS & THE BUSINESS LIFE-CYCLE.

PHASES.

In 1983, when Bill was Kimberly-Clark's vice president of exploratory projects, he began pondering the business life-cycle. He was not alone in this preoccupation as he avidly began collecting opinions from a wide range of management thinkers who were also playing with the anthropomorphic vision of a corporation's process of growth, maturity and, in the vast majority of cases, ultimate senility and death.

(I had discovered, while working for the *Philadelphia Daily News*, that its grand, wedding-cake building occupied the site of the great Baldwin steam locomotive works, the General Motors of its day. And now, there are many within the newspaper business who feared that the daily paper was mired in its mature phase, beset by a host of disruptive technologies and smaller, nimbler competitors for advertising dollars. So, life-cycle was not an academic concept, as far as I was concerned.)

Bill's efforts—a classic example of a maverick excursion into the free range—were conducted with a certain amount of secrecy. As Rose Moss observed in her book: "He would take (the group's) analyses and fit them against his own, almost like someone testing jigsaw puzzle pieces for fit. [Wilson does jigsaw puzzles for fun and has a collection in his basement.]"

It reminded me of many of Bill's most important maverick traits: his penchant for "looking back," derived from his treks through the Ontario woods with Walter Paul; his habitual desire to "blow up a problem" and refit the pieces of the wreckage; his spooky ability to "always say yes," especially to new ideas that might upset his intellectual apple cart.

Before I came to Wisconsin, Bill had shipped me a thick bundle of documents culled from the archive in his basement. Most of it concerned the life-cycle. It still had the look of a work in progress—Bill later told me that he hadn't been able to finish the work before he retired.

The framework for the theory, however, appeared to be strong and clear. It seemed simplicity itself—then grew increasingly layered, complex. First he divided the life-cycle into five stages:

IDEA STAGE: Develop new products based on either technical innovation, strategic innovation or both.

ENTREPRENEURIAL: Gain diversification by establishing a new business based on products fulfilling a basic need in an innovative manner.

GROWTH: Increase market penetration and improve profitability by rapid exploitation of successful entrepreneurial ventures.

SHAKE-OUT: The business attracts many competitors. Prices fall. Winners culled from losers.

EXPANSION: Extend business and build on opportunities. Use as a base to exploit associated opportunities.

MATURE: Harvest the present business. Manage for cash.

"Put these categories into the real world, please," I asked Bill when we sat down with the papers.

"I began to think," he responded, "that if you look at these stages, if you have a good idea and you take it to the entrepreneurial stage—what I used to call, 'Make a little, sell a little'—you have something that you can grow by adding products to the line; you can grow it by rolling it out geographically, that sort of thing. The minute you get to the growth stage, your competition can *see* you. And other people will come in.

"When Kotex started to really roll—and, remember, it was a behind-the-counter product in a plain brown wrapper—when it began to be seen, within two years there were 146 competing products. But after the shakeout period, there were only a half-dozen left."

"I'm thinking that the expansion stage is where you get Kimberly buying Scott," I said.

Bill repeated what he had said back in Tiburon: "Companies do two things in this stage. They buy back their stock. Or they buy their competition. When I see a company buying its stock it says to me they don't have alternatives. Kimberly-Clark never bought-in its stock when they were generating new businesses. Darwin Smith bet the company on the diaper—he needed every penny to market it."

Bill further atomized each stage into two broadly-brushed categories: Management Characteristics and Cultural Characteristics. Each was again broken down into subcategories (for a full account, see Appendix), then broken down again. Mind-boggling.

Now Bill swept his hand across the scattered pages. "If I'd known this when I was back in New Products (*in the early '60s*), I'd have twisted management's tail. I'd have tied it in knots. I would have known exactly where these guys were and how to handle 'em. But I didn't, and I didn't understand this. *This* is the major key. You know exactly where you need people and where you're missing people and what you need to do," he said.

"Shakeout, Expansion, Mature. Those are stages where general and operating managers generally have their experience. Which is why they're like fish out of water when they're forced to innovate—in effect, climb-back up to the Idea and Entrepreneurial stages.

"Mavericks are most effective in the top two stages," Idea and Entrepreneurial. "Business life-cycle helps you to know when to send the maverick out to the free range."

"That's the irony of protecting the maverick," I said. "The maverick who starts something isn't the best person to run it into the Mature stage."

"If you're going to use the maverick properly, you've got to convince 'em to cycle back to the Idea and Entrepreneurial stages and do it all over again. Sometimes, the handoff is easier from one maverick to another. The second maverick can carry the project a little further but, finally, you have to put in a manager. Protecting the maverick often involves convincing the maverick he can't go all the way to the bottom of the chart."

It was Bill's instinct that he had to recycle back up to the Idea and Entrepreneur stages (long before he codified it in his life-cycle work) that made it possible for Bill to hand off the disposable diaper when P&G's Pampers hit the streets in the mid-'60s. The same held true for John Raley's work on Huggies diapers twenty years later.

MORPHING INTO MANAGEMENT.

Sometimes, the maverick doesn't return to the top of the chart. Such was the case of Bill's old maverick-comrade, Darwin E. Smith, Kimberly-Clark's CEO from 1971-1982.

"When Darwin was head of the Legal department," said Bill, "he hired the ultimate maverick, a wild guy, to invent things. He paid him out of his budget. Never brought it into the corporation because it was too wild. But Darwin did that. The head of the *legal* department…"

"...running a bootleg R-and-D operation," I said.

"Absolutely. He really was a maverick."

Bill recalled one of his shenanigans—peeling off a

product that had been turned down by the marketing people and selling rights for it to another company for $75 thousand. Then he turned around and creamed the money back against his research budget.

"I don't think you could do that today with the controls that Smith put in," Bill said ruefully.

"As Darwin went down the business stages, he got trapped," I reasoned. "Maybe it's part of what you call, 'paying the price.' As the maverick goes down the business stages, would it be fair to say that the price goes up?"

"Sure," said Bill. "And the price he pays is losing the ability to be a maverick. That's the price Darwin paid. Kimberly-Clark paid him $6 million a year, but whether that was sufficient compensation or not, I don't know."

"There's an irony there," I said. "Smith looked the other way while you were skimming, but later he made it virtually impossible."

"He knew what I was doing," Bill laughed. "When he got to be CEO and wanted strong centralized financial controls, he knew the whole game."

"But by filling that hole, he deprived himself of the services of other mavericks."

Bill grinned mischievously. "I got around him. Other mavericks should have. Makes it tougher, sure, but it makes it a challenge. The maverick will always rise to a challenge."

Leaders do not choose sides
but rather bring
sides together.

Rev. Jesse Jackson

11.
MOMs.

THE AHA! AT ROUNDTABLE TWO.

It had been an interesting week out there in Bill's bosky little Eden, but now it was time to return to LA. Soon, it spread out below the jetliner's wing: a vast, chaotic drawer-full of jewels tossed across the velvet night. Even though I had lived there for 16 years, the sheer, brutal bigness of the place was intimidating.

Yes, the city was gigantic, just as corporations were big and merciless—but now I had seen that there was a way to play *inside* that giant bulk, exploiting the seams and cracks and fissures that always exist, even in the most seemingly monolithic structures. Despite what it might say on the maverick's little box on the organizational chart, that was truly his or her most essential job: cutting the fence, escaping to free range, living to tell the tale, bringing something wild back to be domesticated in the pasture.

It was a viewpoint worth passing around. That's why I was eager to help Lanny share this good stuff with the folks who were coming to his Second Annual Mavericks Roundtable in San Francisco, paying good money (but hardly enough to cover costs) to hear more about these new ideas.

The first Roundtable, a year before in Tiburon, had been a kind of dry run, attended mostly by Lanny's pals in the consulting game, some old Synectics hands, Leo Shapiro, and one of Lanny's current Kimberly-Clark clients. It had the feeling of a Boston try-out for Broadway. But we hadn't been laughed out of the conference room and, in fact, two or three of the original gang (ones who had paid, even) had re-upped for the second go-round.

We couldn't suspect, as we prepped for the second session, that an amazing and wonderful piece of the puzzle was about to drop into place. Nor should grizzled innovators like Bill and Lanny have been surprised. After all, it's the pursuit of the Great Aha! that keeps these guys going. Nor should it have seemed unusual that we didn't really see this Aha! when it was first proposed. But there it was when we looked later, tucked away neatly on page 18 of the meeting notes, popping up in a somewhat formless discussion of mavericks and how they control the perception of failure.

One of the participants, Andy Zander, an executive at Transgenomic Inc., a biotech startup, remarked that "being the interface between the square peg and the round hole, you taper things a lot."

Then John Raley responded with a question: "What kind of person can do this?" And answered his own query: "A mentor of mavericks. A *MOM*!"

Which, at that moment, was ignored.

But then, a few minutes later, John inserted it back into the conversation: "What type of person is a MOM? How would I recognize one?"

And this time it stuck.

Gene Castellano, who manages special projects for Philadelphia Newspapers (publishers of the *Philadelphia Inquirer* and the *Daily News*), noted, "I'm in the role of MOM at work. You listen to people, interpret others' needs."

"What's the difference between our new-found character and, say, a senior manager?" Lanny asked.

In response, the group built a tidy list:

Manager	Mom
Plan	Plot/ challenge
Organize	Facilitate/ nurture/ fertilize
Lead	Protect/ coach/ cheerlead
Evaluate	Reframing/ change roles
Communicate/ control	"Always say yes."/ Lies

After the conference, Lanny and John (Bill had returned to Tucson) took some time to ponder this new creature.

"One of the difficulties in working with Bill is that he is not only a maverick but he's also a MOM," said Lanny.

But if you look carefully at the MOM, we agreed, you'll find him playing two very distinct roles.

Lanny, again: "One of the MOM's functions is looking out for the maverick, protecting him."

"But what's involved in protecting?" I asked.

John answered, "One of the reasons that I'm kind of a MOM is that people, rightly or wrongly, come to the conclusion that I really want to and can help them and that I won't take away any of the credit for their success. I've also been around long enough that I can offer perspectives from different points of view with the credibility of experiences in different areas. So a MOM is usually a person who has been in the organization quite a while."

Lanny weighed in again. "There's another major role for the MOM: Interacting with the senior executive. Managing upwards. It's the interface, I hate that word, with the executive who knows, maybe only instinctually, that he wants what the Maverick Way can produce. The MOM is someone who can understand and get in there in the muck with the maverick as well as extricate himself from the muck and reframe and reposition what the maverick brings back from the free range and work at the level of the senior executive."

"So, the way that a manager can protect a maverick," I said, "is to make sure that there's a MOM in the picture. If you're a 'person who knows one thing,' as Leo Shapiro says, then you're highly unequipped to do much good for a maverick beyond getting out of the way…"

"…and that's a counter-intuitive move for a manager,"

The MOM gets in the muck with the Maverick.

Lanny laughed. "Basically, you're saying, 'I've got to get this person attached to some other person of power in the organization.' We need to communicate to managers: Here's something you can do so you don't screw up. And that's protect the maverick by helping him find a mentor. *And it ain't you.*"

"But how to find the MOM?" I asked. "I'm looking at that from the standpoint of the CEO, COO, high-level guys who'll get charged up and say, 'Damn, I've got to go get me a MOM.' What do you say to someone in that position?"

"Just as mavericks exist in your organization—you need to find them; you can't train them—your mavericks will lead you to your MOMs," Lanny said.

"And I assume, just as you can only find mavericks, you can't go out and open a MOM's academy," I said.

"I'm reminded of the biblical phrase," said Lanny: "'Many are called but few are chosen.' Bill was called to be a mentor of mavericks. You can't appoint someone."

"It's a compulsion; you're compelled to be a mentor," I said. "It's a subterranean process in an organization. Mavericks are a subterranean species. MOMs are a little more visible but they're subterranean, too. And that's a kind of dilemma:MOMs need to work on the management side and the maverick needs a lot of coverage, secrecy, anonymity, room to maneuver."

"They don't need secrecy," said John. "Otherwise they don't have the power it takes to be a MOM within the organization. But they do need some *mystery*. Bill did a lot of stuff that left others shaking their heads and wondering, 'How did he do that? How did he get permission to do that?'

"The answer is Bill never *asked* for permission."

"MOMs need mystery," John added, "in order to do what they do, otherwise everyone would be doing it and mucking things up for all of us."

"Secrecy is an artifact," said Lanny. "Bill had tremendous faith in allowing a maverick like Hrubecky to play in the free range, that new things were going to happen. In one sense, he believed in the power of revelation, that more will be revealed to those who are willing to extend themselves and venture into the free range.

"As a result of that, it appears to be quite secretive,

because at one stage the maverick and the MOM themselves don't know what's going to happen. But they believe that something good is going to happen.

"Something good *does* happen. Sometimes not when they expected and frequently not where they expected it—it's a surprise. What looks like a secret is really a surprise *before* it has happened."

John and I muttered *Aha!* in the same breath.

WHAT MOM DOES.

"Let's go back," I prompted, "to what you said about the senior executive who likes what the Maverick Way produces. What's at stake?"

"I think the senior executive is frequently not a maverick," Lanny replied. "The interesting thing about Peter Larson (*formerly a Kimberly-Clark executive vice president and, at one key moment, Bill's boss*) is that he recognized that he needed what mavericks could produce. He was looking for more big hits. He knew the way to do that was through what we're calling the Maverick Way. What he didn't know explicitly (but sensed implicitely) is that there was another key element involved and that was MOMs."

"I would put it a little differently," said John. "I'd say that Larson was looking for some big hits and he knew that the normal status quo way of doing things wasn't going to deliver them. He knew he was looking for something different, but he didn't know exactly what it was. And because he didn't know what it was, his actions were intuitive and without the benefit of what we've done the last year or two—stepping back and thinking through the big picture. We are trying to codify this thing—Larson was seat of the pants. No one had gone down that road before."

Larson, we recalled, had challenged Bill to "change the way the company thinks." Out of that came Bill's last position at Kimberly-Clark, head of the Innovation Management team in 1985—the team that numbered among its members Lanny Vincent and John Raley.

"Did Bill really teach others how to think differently?" I asked, having gone through one or two episodes of "changing thinking" at the *Register*—and having seen the staff (myself included) stubbornly resist and, ultimately, wear the brilliant new idea down to a nub.

"I think so," said John.

"The company as a *whole*?" I persisted.

"Yup. We spent a lot of time putting people through training programs on listening to one another more effectively, how to work together as teams, basically changing how people worked together and that's changing the way the company thinks. Bill's group was the entry portal for a lot of new management concepts: world-class manufacturing, value-added management stuff."

"Did it change the way the entire organization called Kimberly-Clark thought?" said Lanny. "No. Did it have an impact? Yes. Did it effect the organization's revenue stream? Yes.

"Bill had a great sensitivity for the edge of the corporation—the leading and bleeding edge. That's where he chose to effect change. He didn't waste time trying to change for change's sake."

John agreed. "Bill sought out parts of the organization that were in pain; they were hurting; they weren't doing as well as they wanted. When the pain of change becomes less than the pain of staying the same, you become more open to looking at new ideas, to changing your thinking. Bill was good at identifying not only what parts of the organization were in pain, but their level of pain and whether they were open to considering a different way."

"Is this intrinsic to the role of the MOM?" I asked.

"It's absolutely essential," said Lanny.

"It's part of the renewal process," said John. "Let's go back to what a maverick's doing. A maverick is trying to bring something from the free range that the corporate pasture will adopt. That will occur easiest in that part of the pasture where people are *looking* for something to adopt. If a part of the corporate pasture is sitting there fat, dumb and happy, you can bring them the best thing since sliced bread and they won't care. So, being able to find those areas of the organization that are in pain helps the MOM direct or steer the maverick in ways that will have a higher probability of acceptance."

"What's the span of control for a MOM?" I asked.

"It's not a span of control, because a MOM isn't controlling," Lanny snapped.

"OK, we're struggling for a new vocabulary," I muttered.

"I do think there *is* a limit," John soothed. "If one assumes that a Bill Wilson can devote one hour a week to a John Raley, that obviously puts an upper limit on how many mavericks Bill Wilson can mentor. So infinite isn't the answer, because that would spread the MOM too thin. At one point in time, Bill was an active MOM to nine people. I can recall several conversations where we felt that we weren't able to get as much of Bill's time as we needed. Whether we really needed it or not is another question."

"Yeah, I would agree," said Lanny. "I think a MOM's span of influence is a function of three things: The maverick-to-mentor ratio, which John's been talking about. Which is limited. The second is the opportunity-to-innovation ratio—even a large corporation like Kimberly-Clark can't handle too many significant, rule-changing innovations at any one time. Third is John's 'pockets of pain.' How much pain is there in the organization? I think the span of influence is a function of those three factors.

The latter two have to do with the MOM's role in extending sponsorship, not just protecting mavericks."

"Say you're Kimberly-Clark's CEO, how would you evaluate a MOM's performance?" I asked. "What tells an upper-level manager, 'This guy is doing good stuff.'"

"Two things," said Lanny. "First, succession. Do we have a cadre of mavericks and budding young MOMs? It's *who's* in development, not what's in development.

"The other is: Do I have more options now for the future of the corporation than I had before? Options to exercise, choices to make."

"How do you compensate a MOM?" I asked.

"I don't think you *can* pay somebody for being a MOM," said John. "I think you're now at a level of freedom where you're beyond compensation."

"Let's ask John the question," Lanny grinned. "Could you be paid more for your MOM activity?"

"Sure, I'll take the raise!" John laughed.

"If you were paid more for your MOM activity," Lanny fired back, "would it mean that you would do more of it?"

"No," said Raley. "What motivates a MOM is the ability—it's span of influence. I feel like I've got more irons in the fire, although they're not *my* irons."

"Do MOMs wear out?" I asked, thinking back to some questions I was forming about Bill's retirement, what I had started calling his "endgame." "I'm getting the feeling that at some point Bill simply wore out."

"I think maybe MOMs are like old soldiers: they never die, they just fade away. That's a flippant answer," Lanny giggled. "Maybe the MOM doesn't wear out, but his relationships aren't as viable as they once were.

"You get a new CEO, you get different players and as soon as that happens, relationships shift. Bill's power and sphere of influence at Kimberly-Clark was tremendous. He probably extended those relationships way beyond their normal life expectancy. So, maybe the question is: How many administrations is a MOM good for?"

"I would argue that a MOM *does* wear out," said John. "Two things are going on here. I believe that most companies have generational cliques. Bill had his generational clique. Wayne Sanders (*Kimberly-Clark's current CEO*) has his generational clique."

"Much to Bill's credit," Lanny interjected, "Bill was able to grow into a new generational clique."

"Bill's *unusual*," John laughed, echoing something Leo Shapiro had said many months before. "Second, as a MOM nurtures mavericks, a lot of those mavericks grow up to become MOMs themselves.

"So the senior MOM doesn't have as strong a role. They pass the baton. They ride off into the sunset, because they're not as needed, pragmatically."

"My instinct," I said, "is that the MOM is the way that

an organization establishes the succession of mavericks. The MOM is the engine that keeps the wheel turning."

"Larson asked Bill the wrong question," Lanny mused. "It wasn't a matter of teaching the organization to be a maverick. It was, 'Can you work out the succession?' What drives MOMs is their interest in keeping the story going."

It was, I recalled, one of the maverick's tools, something that Lanny, true to his theological background, had called the "apostolic succession."

"Where Bill maybe failed—when you ask the question, did he cause the organization to think differently?—is that he concentrated on mavericks and not MOMs," Lanny added. "And what Bill didn't leave was a strong cadre of MOMs. John is probably the only MOM he left behind. Bill did that implicitly, not explicitly. Had Bill had the notion of MOMs, I think he would have done it differently.

"This has fallen into a very powerful piece—renewal via succession, which requires a mentor, a guide, a MOM. Renewal is not just about finding the next new thing. It's also about the MOM who can cultivate mavericks."

"Mavericks give the organization a reason to believe," said John. "Leaving behind a legacy of MOMs gives the organization sustainability."

MOM CLOSER TO HOME.

As this conversation unfolded, I realized with a jolt that there had been a MOM at *The Register*. His name was Jim Robison and he was the managing editor when I joined the paper in 1981. He was a tall, almost saturnine veteran of newspapers here and there (like most of us in this gypsy business). He had been one of the editor's first hires, back when the *Register* was a widely-ridiculed rag with the mighty *Los Angeles Times* breathing down its neck. The paper's turnaround had barely begun when I signed on—you had to be wildly imaginative to see what would happen.

Jim "ran" the place—but, then again, he didn't. He didn't attend the daily news huddle (a sacred institution at most papers, where the top editors gather to plan the day's coverage and pitch stories for major play—in short, a carnival of office politics and ego). In fact, there wasn't really a meeting at all, since as the Duke of Features, I pretty much ran my shop the way I wanted and told Jim about it later—if I remembered to tell him. Which, despite the fact that most editors are ferocious control-freaks, didn't seem to bother him. Instead he would cruise around the newsroom (a pretty small square-footage in those days), mumbling about something or other...just, *there*. Just as Bill had been somewhere... *around*.

I didn't realize it at the time (we were all moving too fast for much introspection back then), but Jim was almost recklessly brave where it counted: in trusting and nurturing the mavericks and crypto-mavericks and would-be mavericks that presented themselves for enlistment on the paper. Given that the *Register* was a tough sell to properly pedigreed journalists, that trust often was stretched to the breaking point.

I recalled an evening when Jim and I interviewed a job candidate over Chinese food at a local low-cost restaurant. We were having a typical courtship conversation as Robison sulkily pushed his egg foo yung back and forth across his plate.

The young woman smiled brightly and said, "Jim, if you don't eat your dinner we'll give it to you in an enema."

Jim and I promptly, happily, hired her. And she turned out to be one heck of a designer—and, I now realized, one heck of a maverick whose ways drove the more conventional players in the place nuts. She once snuck through a Food section cover illustration of a long, lithe female leg, shod in a stilleto heel which was, in turn, poised ever-so-delicately on top of an egg yolk. The headline, which she also wrote: "Whip them, beat them, but respect them in the morning."

The editor was not amused. Until the cover started raking in awards.

Robison went along as I began assembling the new features staff from places far beyond the normal hiring pool: the editor of a rock 'n' roll alternative weekly, a PR guy from the San Francisco opera, a fellow who traded electric guitars for a living, one of the copyboys who wound tapes for the old linotype machines. Jim bought them all.

And then Robison's cobbled-together news operation won a Pulitzer Prize. Which set off a wild, day-long celebration that trashed the newsroom, cheap champagne sloshing over our shoe tops and screwing up the comput-

ers. But, even in the midst of the revelry, Jim and I agreed that there was something a little sad going on, too—now we were a "serious" newspaper.

"In ten years they'll be rebelling against all this," he opined.

How true…

Jim lasted another year or so, then left for another job and we gradually fell out of touch. But now I was thinking back to my experiences with him. Now they made sense.

He was a MOM.

And me? Had I missed my best shot at being a maverick?

Leaders cannot be trained, but they can be educated.

Richard Farson

12.
ENDGAME.

You can't be a Maverick if your successors are rubber stamp copies.

'TEACH THE CORPORATION TO DO WHAT YOU DO.'

There was one last, unfinished piece of business for Lanny, Bill and me: an exploration (and, hopefully, resolution) of something that had been gnawing at us since the earliest days of our journey together.

I called it "the endgame," the final half-decade of Bill Wilson's years at Kimberly-Clark—ironically his best and (I suspected) also his most frustrating years.

It had started with Bill moving from Energy & Environment, where he was parked (perhaps too harsh a word) after being pulled out of the company's troubled European operation in 1977, to his redesign of a major chunk of the corporate structure (that, essentially, left him without a job) and his invitation from the Kimberly-Clark executive whose staff he had flattened to "do what you do best."

His one-man operation—"I was a lone wolf," said Bill—first fell into orbit around Kimberly-Clark executive Leroy Peterson, who was in charge of K-C's mills, engineering and research operations. He, in turn, reported to K-C Executive Vice President Peter Larson.

Bill's self-designed new job now meant that Kimberly-Clark *itself* was Bill's free range. He had carte-blanche to snoop wherever he pleased, looking for problems—nothing less than John Raley's "pockets of pain"—spotting interesting ideas, collecting his little herd.

"A lot of the managers hated me," Bill recalled with a

laugh. "When they saw me coming, they'd cringe. But some of them, if they were in trouble, kinda welcomed me. Because I did swing some weight. I could command assistance, get research or engineers from another area to come in and look at the problem."

It was in a meeting with Larson that Bill was asked if he could "teach the corporation to do what you do."

And, of course, Bill answered yes.

Now the question presented itself—why had Larson issued that challenge to Bill? I tracked Larson down: he's currently the chairman and chief executive of the Brunswick Corp., the sporting-goods manufacturer (everything from Flexible Flyer sleds to Zebco reels). I wrote him a letter requesting an interview.

After a week or so, I got a reply:

> "Dear Richard:
>
> "While I greatly appreciate your letter, I am afraid that I don't have much to add and am awfully busy. So, here's my view of what happened:
>
> "1. Kimberly-Clark had developed a 'stodgy' view of R&D, since its cost to implement in paper/ tissue tended to come in $100-million capital units.
>
> "2. My view was that we needed to liven up Kimberly-Clark's R&D if we were going to effectively compete (and win) against P&G

(which I viewed as a mechanical, engineering company).

"3. As an undergraduate physics student, I gained an appreciation for those who 'see' things (products) that others could not envision and which could not be mathematically defined with precision at the outset. I also learned something about the difference between the true individual innovators whose ideas were generally unsupported at the outse, but had sound concepts underlying their views, as contrasted to the intellectually disorderly individuals who generally produced nothing important. This view was affirmed and strengthened during my time in the nuclear submarine Navy.

"4. My initial contact was with Fred Hrubecky, who I came to respect and learned of his respect for Bill Wilson as his mentor. Thus, when we set out to produce 'practical magic,' Bill's role as a mentor and his previous successes made his leadership role a natural.

"5. The 'fuel' was expense money and the 'matches' were (1) giving them a proud title—the 'legitimate crazies,' and (2) meeting with them regularly (which, of course, they spread around K-C) to cause them to judge/ prioritize their own projects. The bottom line is that talent is hard to find and funding practical innovators (in heavy metal corporations which tend to avoid risk) is one of the great joys of management. That's my story and I'm going to stick to it!

"Sincerely,

"Peter"

The letter answered a few questions—and prompted a bunch more. So, going into my best journalistic whine-mode, I wrote back what I hoped was a properly unctuous letter asking a number of follow-up questions. I posted the letter. A week or so later, the phone rang. It was Peter Larson.

With hardly a pause for opening pleasantries (beyond saying that he didn't want to reply by e-mail because it made his "fingers bleed"), he launched directly into the subject at hand: managing a maverick, the top-down view.

"The thing I liked about Bill was that when I talked to him about (*creating the Exploratory Projects group*), he understood. And, frankly, he was old enough and experienced enough and had seen enough things go up and down that he set out to do it in a way that didn't make every other word a reference to the authority that I had given him."

What Bill understood is that Larson wanted him to assemble a team of what he called "legitimate crazies."

"So," I asked, "how'd he do on that score?"

"He was magnetic," said Larson. "They followed him around like the Pied Piper of Hamlin.

"He used the money, he built the team, and the team pushed the ideas. We had a little group of people who got together once a month and talked about the good ideas that were floating around.

"Then I could reach down from the top when I was talking to a division leader and I could say to him, 'I understand you guys got a back-room project going on.' And, of course, the guy didn't know. So he'd admit he didn't know and then he'd go around and start checking and pretty soon he was spending a fair amount of time on what was going on out there. And he knew there was a level of enthusiasm for new ideas coming from the top. In effect, the divisions became the meat in the sandwich."

I asked Larson how he had kept his fingers in the Innovation Management pie.

"I monitored Bill's performance more from listening to the division guys and offering feedback to Bill on the places where he had issues and needed to make courtesy calls and bring people in. Frankly, I was doing a little coaching on the psychology side of selling, which was not always Bill's great strength."

I probed that last remark.

"I think I had Bill pretty well judged up front," said Larson, "and what I learned is that zealots often don't take the time to appropriately package their message. At the end of the day, that may be the thing that most adversely affects their productivity. So you've got to help them do that.

"Bill, for example, would go into a cerebral popcorn session and he'd be kind of light on the instructions. And he wouldn't see the political value of getting an audience that went beyond the people he thought were legitimate crazies.

"I think all zealots believe that their proposition is inherently simple and obvious. And so, particularly in the area of innovation, they don't stop to check that everybody is coming along with them. Particularly the power players.

"Bill always thought that the operating guys were a little stupid. And that's a bad way to look at people. It produces all kind of secondary impacts that are relatively unattractive. As differentiated from saying, 'I think you're a really smart guy and I understand that you come at this from a different angle, so let me help you see this the way I see it and maybe I'm off a little bit…' Bill was not always good at self-depreciating humor. He was a genuine zealot."

"You and he talk about that?" I asked.

"I would kid him about it. For a man of his age and experience the cement was pretty well hardened. I don't mean this in a negative way, but he was the only guy I had. So, you do what you can. I don't mean that to sound negative. Bill was a package of talent. But we generally fail not over our strengths but over our weaknesses."

"Were you aware of what Bill calls his 'lying, stealing and cheating?'"

"Sure. I would have been disappointed if he hadn't."

"How did you work with that?"

"I looked the other way."

"When did you *not* look the other way? What would trigger that?"

"The financial guys would come in and bitch about it. And, every once in a while a division guy would bitch about it. And so, I knew it was going on. And I felt that in this case ignorance was bliss and highly productive."

"Did you have a sense that Bill needed that to function?"

"Well, 'need' is a very strong word," said Larson. "Did I think he enjoyed doing it—yes. Did it facilitate his attitude in general? Absolutely."

"If you have a guy who is lying, stealing and cheating," I asked, "how can you trust him?"

"It depends on *when* they were lying, stealing and cheating," Larson responded. Developing concepts was one thing, he added, but, ultimately the new products that resulted had to pass muster with the consumer in test markets. "So in effect there was a stopper that kept totally crazy ideas that had no relevance to the consumer from getting through."

"What was Bill's batting average on moving things through that pipeline?" I asked.

"I think you've got to count it by two measures," said Larson. "First, you have to count it in terms of products... and I'd say he was hitting north of .300. But, again, I think the real value is in places where you couldn't measure it and attribute it directly to Bill's influence. The other R-and-D operations, with 100 times the people, got the message.

"Which was?"

"Think out of the box. Be in front of the consumer, who if you go out and ask them will be unable to tell you in many cases what they need next."

BRANDING THE MAVERICK.

The worm at the core of the apple was this: Granting the wonders of hindsight, had Peter Larson fatally "branded" Bill when he asked him to "teach the corporation to do what you do?"

Had Larson, unwittingly, pulled Wilson-the-Maverick out of his subterranean system of tunnels and trapdoors and escape hatches and made him public. *Too public?* John Raley had alluded to that fear earlier, when he noted that branding the maverick gives an organization potentially fatal "targeting information."

And, rest assured, there *were* players in K-C's upper reaches who had targeted Bill. As he recalled several times over the course of our conversations, "Five years after I retired I heard a story about an executive vice president and a couple of other vice presidents going in to *(Kimberly-Clark CEO)* Darwin Smith, wanting to get me out of their hair.

"Darwin listened very politely. And when they were finished he tilted his chair back and put his feet on his desk and said, 'Look, you guys. When any one of you has developed as many processes and new products and new businesses for this corporation as Wilson has, you can have a job for life, just like he's got. Now get the hell out of my office.'"

What to make of that story? Bill, as always, refused to supply an easy moral. The first couple of times I heard it, I marked it down as an old warrior's tale of triumph over the corporate foe. But now it didn't seem so simple. To me, or to Lanny.

It was hindsight again, but we were beginning to feel that Smith, arguably Kimberly-Clark's canniest, most visionary CEO, had erred in his reputed response. Yes, in a sense he was "protecting" the maverick, but at the price of failing the MOM. Or, more accurately, failing to fully understand the implications of "teaching the corporation to do what you do." Because if there were any dons of the organization that needed to be taught, they were sitting across from Darwin Smith's desk.

Of course, no one (Bill included) had conceptualized

any of this MOM stuff—and even if they had, they might not have taken it as more than mumbo jumbo. But, then again, I had seen how the awareness of "mavericks" and "MOMs" had altered my view of what I did—and what others did. It hadn't changed the facts but it had powerfully changed how I reacted to them.

Now we could conceive of another scenario back in Darwin Smith's office: an invitation to those corporate bulls to open up their part of the pasture and start cultivating some MOMs.

But it didn't happen.

FINDING A 'SAFE POSITION.'

There were jarring changes in Bill's working situation in those last years. With Darwin Smith's retirement looming, the executive suite started churning. Smith rotated Larson from marketing to manufacturing duties, swapping him with another executive VP, Richard Sonnentag. So, just like *that*, Bill had a new boss.

"Bill had an impression that Sonnentag was a bean counter," said Lanny. "He came from a financial background, didn't really understand all this stuff and therefore Bill was very cautious with Sonnentag and very one-on-one with him. But I'll bet Bill would say that he worked better with Sonnentag than with anyone else."

To which Bill readily agreed. Sonnentag essentially

left Bill with Larson's commission and changed just one thing: the name of the group. It was now Innovation Management.

Bill had now been at Kimberly-Clark for two generations. He had, he said, long planned to hang it up when he turned 65. After all, he had his farm and gems and tractors and tin soldiers and a couple of gentleman-entrepreneur businesses on the side. He wanted to "play."

"We knew that once Bill retired nobody was going to succeed him, *could* succeed him," said Lanny. "Nobody thought Bill's group would last as long as it did. We gave it three years—it actually lasted for at least seven years, twice as long as anybody really expected."

Now, Bill started pondering something new, troubling. "Working in Kimberly-Clark you had to be on your toes and watch the political scene," said Bill, "so that you knew how to play things. In Innovation Management, I did more of that than when I was just Exploratory Projects, on my own. Now I had people to run interference for and to try to look after. I was trying to find what I would call 'safe positions' for the members of the Innovation Management group. That took a lot of time, maneuvering."

Lanny was being pressured to go to work for the corporation's Human Resources groups—one of Bill's most implacable bureaucratic foes.

"H-R wanted me to run a training program," said

Lanny. "I was resisting going to work for this group. Bill said, 'You could go to work for this guy and still be, you know, working on my stuff.' I didn't like the feel of that at all."

"It's the old Tomahawk game," I said as Bill chuckled wordlessly.

"So then I decided to leave and go to work for Synectics," said Lanny. "That was when, in parting, Bill said, 'We haven't finished our work together.' It was like a teacher saying, 'Before you can graduate you have to turn in your final paper.' That was the feeling I got. It was transmitted in an instant."

Bill nodded in agreement, but said nothing—the old, familiar waiting game.

"What's a safe position?" Lanny asked, clearly still troubled that Bill had been willing to deal him to a foe.

"A position where they could exercise the background, experience and knowledge that they had gained," said Bill. *Here we go again,* I thought. *We're about to take a sharp detour...*

And, indeed, Bill launched into a long recital of the corporate politics of that moment, a brawl between Sonnentag and one of his executives that led to the shutdown of the New Products operation.

"I still don't make the connection with what *you* did," Lanny needled.

Bill got as cross as I'd ever heard him: "Hang on!

Wait a minute until I paint the picture!" Then off again into a discussion of Darwin Smith breaking up the corporation and rearranging the pieces, a big debate about dedicated versus diversified manufacturing, Sonnentag being posted to Europe (Bill kept him as his boss, even though that meant reporting to someone in London).

All of which told us—nothing. The old fox.

"How did you fit into that?" Lanny asked again.

"It didn't make much difference how I would fit in, because I knew I was leaving," said Bill. He'd wriggled away yet again.

"Let me pose this to you," said Lanny, yanking Bill back to the mid-'80s. "This is a time when Darwin realized that he was at the end of his 20-year sprint to transform Kimberly-Clark from a forest-products to a consumer packaged business. You were a contemporary of Darwin's. Your efforts to innovate were absolutely critical, key, seminal for Darwin's success. Though your contributions were never heard of…"

"Right."

"…but absolutely seminal. No one could escape the timing of your retirement. Yes, it was planned. But, also, this was the end of an era."

"Darwin retired two years after I did," Bill muttered.

"So, you had been involved in two pregnant times of change in Kimberly-Clark's evolution. In one sense, you didn't fit in the future and you recognized that. And in one sense you fit in so well and were so necessary to Darwin that there was a completeness and appropriateness, a kind of symmetry in what was happening. True?"

"I think so."

"Did Kimberly-Clark want you to stay?" Lanny persisted.

"Yes. Sonnentag asked me five times to stay."

"What did he want you to do?"

"Continue doing what I was doing."

"Why didn't you agree?"

"I felt that I'd done it," Bill answered. "If they weren't going to accept it now, staying another year or two wasn't going to change a thing."

"What's the '*it,*' Bill?" I asked.

"They didn't accept the fact that these guys could do it—give them the chance. They said, 'We don't believe it.'"

"You couldn't have been surprised by that response. You'd been getting it for 42 years at Kimberly-Clark," I said.

"True. And that's why I said staying another two years wasn't going to change anything," said Bill with a triumphant chuckle.

I tried to put a rope around the old maverick: "You, of all people, would know that mavericks are going to make it no matter what. The kiss of death is for a maverick to be branded. And yet you were concerned that the company wouldn't brand these guys."

"I was pissed off that they wouldn't give them a chance," Bill grumbled.

"But a maverick makes his *own* chances."

"I didn't care if they anointed them," said Bill. "I wanted to put them in a position where they could utilize their background, experience, knowledge. Then I knew they would be successful."

"But that leads to the question: How do you launch these guys? If you're a MOM, do you want them to be, in your terms, given a chance? or do you want to instruct them on the ways that mavericks hollow out their own space inside an organization? Raley says you flew 40-thousand-foot cover and kept torpedoes away from his waterline. That's different than going to Sonnentag and saying, This guy Raley deserved X, Y and Z."

"You don't do that," said Bill patiently. "Fred Hrubecky makes the point that it's very important that a maverick has a place to run to. You can shove them out or they'll go out on their own—but they need to know that they can run to a safe haven."

"There's another dimension to the question," said Lanny. "The organization's dimension. The irony that I hope we don't miss—and from Bill's tone of voice I can pick up some disappointment—is that he had been asked to prepare people and he had to fight really hard to find them a safe place. And I think that what Bill's saying is,

The fact that I had to fight so hard to find them a safe place rather than have somebody beating the door down to get them for their group was disappointing. Which leads to the question: How do you actually transfer the maverick way between generations?

"This is where Kimberly-Clark failed Bill and failed itself. It did not successfully transfer the intellectual capital about innovation and its management. It failed to transfer that to the next generation. I'm not sure why. Maybe there was too much of a generation gap. So, perhaps the endgame truly is the succession question. And where Kimberly-Clark fell down is that they couldn't build the structure—although maybe we haven't given John Raley credit.

"Maybe Bill *has* succeeded. On the one hand, it wasn't done formally. But of course the maverick way is *never* done formally. So, you could argue the other side of the street.

"Now, is Wayne Sanders (*Kimberly-Clark's current CEO*) aware of this? Probably not.

"And that's what's disappointing to Bill. That's what we hear in his tone of voice: at the upper level, the senior guys didn't protect this important renewal gene. It was left to atrophy, to work out on its own.

"Which, because it's so resilient, it can. But it could be so much more."

MEANWHILE, BACK AT THE RANCH.

This conversation was cast against the backdrop of what was happening in my own little drama at the *Register*. As we pondered "endgame," I realized that I might just be in the midst of my own. And that somehow, in some mysterious way, Bill (and Lanny and the others) had shifted the props and the scenery and the drama itself. Whether it would be comedy or tragedy I couldn't tell.

Maybe it was both.

To set the scene some recapitulation is in order: Back in 1991, N. Christian Anderson, the paper's topmost editor, had turned the newsroom upside down and created something called "the newsroom without walls." He had given me a new job—managing editor for strategy and administration, which was basically a one-man operation that would... well, here it gets a little vague. Run strategic planning, serve as a foil for the newsroom's notoriously short attention-span, do research—it was a moving target of a job.

It had not been a good fit. Gradually, the "strategy" stuff withered and, finally, I was given responsibility for the Sunday paper, although I retained some vestiges of the old job—less functions than a new attitude, one that I wouldn't fully understand until I met Bill. When I did, I realized that my strange job had probably been influenced by Bill and Innovation Management more than anyone or anything else, through his connections with Lanny and Synectics—the old Mobius strip.

Now, knowing how Bill had done that sort of formless, free-floating job—off and on for four decades, no less!—I now understood all too well where I had failed.

And where the *Register* had failed, as well.

I recalled a conversation with the new editor's right-hand man. I told him that I was working on an interesting book, about folks we were calling "mavericks."

I asked him if he thought there were any mavericks around the newsroom. He looked me in the eye and, in a funereal tone, said one word: "No." His voice betrayed not the slightest note of regret.

He was right. In the decade since the "newsroom without walls," I had watched the people I now would call mavericks leave, one by one, many of them people I had hired in the early, manic-desperation days of the paper's turnaround. That was then: we had to take risks or leave desks empty. This was now: we were getting resumes from people at the *Washington Post,* for heaven's sake. We now had what every other big-time newspaper in the country possessed: a restless, nomadic staff of hired guns, each properly certified by an institution of higher learning and suitable two-year stints at increasingly larger, more prestigious papers.

The *Register*, we reminded ourselves more often than necessary, was "better" in every way. We even had the

Pulitzers and other assorted icons of industry self-congratulation to prove it. We saw other papers copying our stuff—most of all the behemoth up the road in LA.

But could you sneak around behind the machinery and occasionally slip a spanner into the well-oiled gears?

Could you pinch the beast without getting body-slammed in response? Don't ask.

My work with Bill and Lanny had left me with a vague sense, not of failure, but of missed opportunities.

"If there had been a Bill Wilson in that operation I certainly would have found him. He would have found me, and we would have done some interesting things," I told Lanny.

"So," he replied, "if we have a message for the *Register*, it's, 'You blew it. You had a maverick. You needed a MOM.'"

TO BE, OR NOT?

As the research phase of the book wound down, I was also finishing up work on a proposal that had been prompted by the current editor's vision (if that's the right word) of the newspaper as a "platform" for launching scads of other informational enterprises. Done on the cheap, of course, by "recycling" the millions of words published on newsprint into magazines, pamphlets, Internet sites, you name it.

Books? A no-brainer. I started researching the economics of the book industry, looking at *Register* material that might fit between boards. If you cut a few corners, kept the press runs low, you could produce books for amounts of capital that were chump change to a big organization like the *Register*.

In fact, I *had* some chump change, money sitting in the bank from profits on a yearly writer's conference the paper sponsored and that I managed. It was tucked away, not quite off the books,considered seed money for the next year's conference, but the money never came close to being spent.

What had Bill called it? "Creaming" profits from one area and, without so much as a heads-up, using it to launch something new.

I had a formal, written proposal sitting in my desk drawer, ready to be launched at the newsroom's top management, to be discussed and debated and evaluated and analyzed and re-submitted and, probably, lost in the shuffle of some immediate crisis in the news. It was a pattern I had seen repeated many times before.

Without calling Bill, I knew precisely what he would advise me to do (although he would offer that advice by telling me a story).

He would tell me a yarn about his adventures "making a little, selling a little."

He would tell me a story about not "seeking permission but forgiveness." He would tell me about how he had covered up a project that had bombed, maybe even one he had blown up himself.

He would tell me about lying, stealing and cheating. About collecting. About projects he had developed, then dropped like a hot potato so he could charge back onto the free range.

I sat in my office and pondered this. I also pondered the implications of a form letter I had received from the company's Human Resources department. It told me that, after 16 years of company service, I could now… retire.

I would get a relative pittance every month but it would leave a few bucks left over after the mortgage. My wife, bless her, thought I was nuts to keep hauling my frustrations home from the paper.

I pondered this, and the fact that I wanted very, very badly to write this book and other books as well. I knew that I could pull off the book project and that in launching it, I would launch myself on the maverick's dangerous, exhilarating trajectory, but I also knew that, sooner or later, management would hunt me down. I had seen it happen too many times before; I had been a participant in too many of the necktie parties.

I could be a maverick. But the place had been scoured clean of MOMs.

So, I did two things: I pulled out the *Register* book proposal and submitted it to the editor.

Her response, after a week or so, was completely predictable: "Not now. Maybe later. We'll let you know."

Then I quit.

And I wrote *"The Maverick Way."*

The real voyage
of discovery
consists not in
seeking new
landscapes but
in having
new eyes.

Marcel Proust

13.
THE MAVERICK WAY.

ENDINGS AND BEGINNINGS AND ENDINGS AND...

It had been quite a journey from Lanny's white-on-white shoebox office above Sam's Bar in Tiburon; from my discovery of a word, if not a concept, to Bill's wordless unfolding of the paper in his wallet; to Tucson and the *skritch-skritch* brainstorming that led us to free range and pasture, to fences and farmers; to the secret society of "legitimate crazies," both past and present; to discovering the mysterious ways of MOMs—and the endgame: Lanny's, Bill's, mine.

Lanny and I had changed, each in our own way. And wasn't that what we had been seeking all along? Ironically, the person who seemed to have changed the least was Bill himself. And yet, externally, his life had changed the most, fate taking some nasty hops as our project wound down. He lost his oldest son, surely one of life's cruelest blows for a parent. (Bill didn't tell me; I heard it from one of his friends—in fact, Bill only mentioned the death once, simply as something that had happened, no emotional context to it at all.)

In the winter, he had quadruple bypass heart surgery and a difficult recovery, his voice breathless, wheezing at the other end of the 1,700-mille connection.

The closest he came to a complaint was his admission that "I'm weak as a kitten." But he said it with no more outward emotion than he would use in describing a chemical reaction. It was simply, starkly the way things *were*. In that sense, Bill's core—his solidity, his "emotional IQ," as Lanny had called it—remained stubbornly, triumphantly, the same.

I marveled at my emotions when I heard about Bill's medical problems. I had come to love the guy, but I still wasn't sure *why*. Bill and I had never really exchanged intimate personal revelations; he was always willing to answer my nagging questions, but he retained a calm distance, a watchfulness, a wariness that hadn't changed much since our first meeting in the Marin county restaurant. He had never offered me advice—probably wouldn't have had I asked; had never pushed me in one direction or another in any of his early readings of the book, beyond an infuriating tendency to make nit-pick copy-edits.

And yet he had, without question, changed my life. How did he do it? Damned if I know. It's the final, ultimate mystery at the heart of the Maverick Way. Bill was like a catalyst in one of his beloved chemical equations—changing something without being itself altered. A mystery: not intended, not manufactured, but… just the way it *is*.

Lanny and I kept coming back to this as we took our last whacks at the Maverick Way.

"Bill's helping me figure out the future, or get closer to seeing what's already there," said Lanny.

"Boy, that's the problem, isn't it?" I agreed. "It's there all along, but *seeing* it is the trick."

Maybe that was the key to the maverick's strange ability to serve as a catalyst—that spooky ability to look at the same reality that presented itself to everyone and organize it, name it, arrange it just a heartbeat sooner.

"Bill opened the maverick way to me," said Lanny, "when he challenged me to do the trends project. 'Go find out before everyone else what the hell's going on.' Dick Loescher opened the maverick way in my first interview when he said, 'We need more interpreters.' He opened the way. That's the key."

"So, if you're Peter Larson and you have it all to do over," I asked, "how would you have handled the transaction with Bill? If he had had the concept of MOM in his head, as opposed to, 'OK. Be a manager, teach the whole corporation.'"

Lanny pondered that a moment: "He might say, 'Find me some mavericks and mentor them and every once in a while you and I will talk about how they're coming along, so we know where they are. And we need to know where your successor is, because we're going to need another MOM.' His challenge should have been: 'As important as the successor to Darwin Smith is the question of the successor to Bill Wilson.'

"MOMs are passionately interested in succession," Lanny continued. "It's not a matter of 'leaving a legacy.' They're not ego-centric. This is where love—agape, selfless love—comes in."

"You can't be a maverick if your successors are rubber-stamp copies," I said.

"Right. And you can't make the Maverick Way into a formula. Any time it gets applied as a formula, it will fail. Because it's explicit and that's too harsh a climate for the Maverick Way. Woe unto you who would try to make this a formula."

"Those who don't understand it aren't looking for a better way," I said.

"That's exactly right," said Lanny. "They're looking for something that they can control or something that'll help their career. So, my advice to them is, don't read this book. It'll be a waste of time."

"More importantly, don't let anyone *else* read it," I laughed.

"The Maverick Way is an affair of love. It's a love of freedom. It's not an affair of control. Maybe that's the last question—Are you part of this secret society? If you are, what will you do? Now that you know the Maverick Way, do you follow it? Are you ready to go?"

Lanny and I looked at one another. Then we said what Bill had been saying all along…

"Saddle up!"

Work can be
approached obliquely
as well as directly.

Robert Townsend

AFTERWORDS.

John Raley: 'Carrying the Torch.'

Passing the torch (the succession question) begs a more important question: do you have a torch to pass? Or better yet, do you have a torch at all?

I believe it is critical that every organization seeking to have an enduring presence must recognize the need to renew itself. The premise of this book is that such renewal relies upon having a few mavericks and a mentor of mavericks (MOM); sometimes more, sometimes fewer mavericks, but *always* a MOM. It is these who will identify new opportunities and cause the organization to grow faster and more profitably than its competitors. Otherwise, if you keep doing what you have always been doing, all you will get is what you already have.

My experience with traditional approaches to the succession question is that these approaches rely on tools and techniques that don't work with mavericks. For example, if you want a finance person, you look for a person with a finance background. If you want a marketing person, you look for someone with a marketing background.

But what qualifies as *maverick* credentials?

A maverick will have an unusually broad spectrum of experiences and interests and can be working in almost any functional area. In order to successfully roam the free range and identify new items of potential value to an organization, the maverick must have the ability to see things from a wide variety of simultaneous points of view: technical, marketing, management, legal, etc. A broad range of experiences and interests prepares the maverick for this.

In my own case, I have a degree in chemical engineering with one course short of also having a minor in physical chemistry; I have published papers on the topic of molecular structures; I have been a disk jockey and personnel manager at a radio station; I have patents in papermaking, nonwoven processes, and absorbent structures; I have worked in R&D, in management consulting and international business management; I have lectured at graduate schools. Marketing people seek my advice; intellectual property attorneys (patents and trademarks) call me a "closet lawyer." I have season tickets to a performing arts theater; tickets to an annual country music festival; I attend stock car races and participate in a water ski show team.

This range of experiences and interests enables the maverick to meaningfully interact with the organization's varied functional areas. Mavericks are chameleons who can change their "colors" and effectively work with the different functional areas of an organization to bring back to the organization what they have found on the free range.

For executives, the nature of the maverick's broad

range of experiences and interests offers a challenge. In a world where management likes to assign people to specific functional areas and career paths, how do you classify the maverick? The challenge will drive the typical human resources manager mad. They will declare the maverick an organizational misfit.

Seeking these misfits, as deemed by personnel, is a good way for the executive to get a head start in finding a maverick.

More difficult and more important is the mentor of mavericks, or MOM. These people are typically more senior and/or tenured in an organization. Almost all of them were, at one time or another, mavericks themselves.

How to discover a MOM? Follow the mavericks. They'll almost always lead you to their corporate MOMs. If you are serious about the long-term renewal of your corporation, it is critical that you have a MOM.

Without a mentor, a maverick will either become a cog in the organizational wheels or he will leave the organization to pursue his or her dreams elsewhere. The mentor of mavericks is a key role for smoothing the maverick's rough edges, and in calming the sometimes stormy organizational waters that the maverick leaves in his wake.

Passing the torch, when it comes to mavericks, is a different problem than than most corporations encounter in their succession planning. Typical succession planning involves identifying someone with excellence in a particular functional area and grooming that person to move higher up the ladder in that functional area.

But the diverse nature of the maverick's interests, experiences and competencies does not lend itself to a content-specific definition of passing the torch. Focusing on a specific content aspect is also counter to the fact that when they're out on the free range, the maverick does not know what will be found, so the maverick (and MOM) must be prepared for diversity.

In a similar vein, passing the maverick torch is not a context issue. When out on the free range, the maverick may find a new product, a new process, a new management technique, a new business opportunity, etc. Just as the specific content of what the maverick will bring back cannot be predicted, the *context* is also impossible to define. That's because passing the torch in the Maverick Way is process-based. The person passing the torch has to identify potential mavericks who would be comfortable exploring the free range. And the person receiving the torch must be comfortable working with many different functional areas.

The foundation of everything a maverick does is the question "How to?" When the maverick finds something in the free range, the question is "How to bring an innovation back?" When brought back to the organization, the question is "How to get each functional area on-board?"

These "How to?" questions indicate that a maverick's role is a matter of process, not content or context. For this reason, passing the torch is a matter of looking for people with the correct attitude, tone, and approach and not necessarily a mastery of a functional skill area.

However, when the question is the MOM's succession, passing the torch is more like a bride tossing her bouquet. The bride does not hand the bouquet to a specific woman, but tosses the bouquet toward the group eligible to catch it. No one knows who, if anyone, will catch the bouquet.

Passing the torch is a matter of accepting the uncertainty and just letting it happen. You never know who will catch the MOM's torch when it is passed. It may even morph into a new area of opportunity in which the Maverick Way is applied much differently than the previous MOM might have envisioned. Just as we cannot clone a maverick, we cannot clone a MOM.

Did Bill Wilson pass the torch to me? I don't think so. Like the bride at the wedding, he gathered a small group of people who were potentially capable, then tossed the torch and trusted that someone would catch it. Bill could not make clones of himself, for in doing so, the Maverick Way would have become a formulated copy and would not have lived.

I believe that I *did* catch the torch that Bill tossed. But, as one would expect from a maverick, it was applied in a different way. Bill applied the Maverick Way to lead Kimberly-Clark into new products and new business areas. I used the Maverick Way to grow an existing small business into a large core part of Kimberly-Clark.

After working with Bill, I was assigned to international operations where I had staff responsibility for a very small unit—the commercial business unit— that was not deemed to be a core business for the corporation. Many times we referred to ourselves as the company's unadopted stepchild.

In 1987, global net sales outside North America and Western Europe for the commercial business unit were less than $35 million a year. Seven years later, sales were about $270 million and comparable in size to the North American and European businesses. To accomplish this required starting many new business units in countries around the world.

I am convinced that my success in starting all these new businesses in a variety of cultures and places has more to do with my application of the Maverick Way as a *process* than the functional skills of my engineering education.

Following this assignment, I have applied the principles of the Maverick Way to establish strategies for global management of Kimberly-Clark patents and trademarks. These new strategies are enabling Kimberly-Clark to have a stronger intellectual property portfolio that is more effectively managed. And in the process, these new strategies are saving millions of dollars each year and these savings will grow significantly over the next decade

In addition to my intellectual property responsibilities, I have now also been asked to lead the accelerated growth of our commercial business unit in Japan. Success will come from applying the Maverick Way to bringing new ideas and new approaches to the business and helping them integrate these into their existing operations.

FRED HRUBECKY: 'A MAVERICK IN DIAPERS.'

In all candor I was surprised to receive a job offer from Kimberly-Clark. As a native of Neenah I knew that the company was only interested in those who graduated at the top of their class. I had graduated from the University of Wisconsin, Madison, in May, 1960, with a degree in mechanical engineering. I was dead last in my class because I subscribed to the weird notion that my professors did not have the only right answers to their questions.

My first job was on Convertors Incorporated, which Bill Wilson created to protect the largest market for Kaycel, the surgical packs business. Because of that experience, I was ruined forever for becoming a staid corporate employee.

Our team was then ensconced at the Ulrich building, an old car dealership in Oshkosh. It became Kimberly-Clark's first skunk works. The atmosphere was very relaxed but very high voltage. No attention was paid to time worked. We all put in many extra hours because we loved it.

However, once or twice a week, I would make a break for the door when the phone rang at 4 p.m. It was Wilson with another idea for a product. I would invariably get the assignment.

Only once was I able to beg off and that was when I went through the market analysis for "Styptic Tissue." This was never going to be a market for a sleeping giant like Kimberly-Clark. Years later I realized that Wilson generated projects like that to draw fire away from the important stuff he was bootlegging.

HOW I DEVELOPED THE DISPOSABLE DIAPER.

After working on pillow cases, Destroylette bags (liners for an incinerating toilet) and record jackets, I was assigned to work on disposable diapers. The marketing types demanded that it sell for three cents (then the cost of diaper service) and be flushable. I went to the patent files and found several designs that were rectangular pads that fit in a rubber pant with two straps that held each end in place. We had a commode at the lab that could have successfully flushed away a dog, so I had the proper test site.

Meanwhile, the tissue group had developed an oiled baby tissue. Neenah Paper Company sold a diaper liner. It was a high wet-strength sheet, perfumed to smell like baby powder.

One of the market researchers designed a coordinated group of packages (in pink and blue, what else?) and we put the products into a market test in Rochester, Binghamton and Syracuse, New York. The test was a flop.

It was decided we needed an outside viewpoint. That was to be provided by Leo Shapiro, one of the most perceptive people I have ever met. Leo would stop customers in the baby section and ask them what was in our boxes. We quickly discovered that almost no one knew what we were selling and this included the sales clerks.

Later that month we came down to Shapiro & Associates in Chicago and Leo proposed we find out what was really needed in a diaper. Leo's plan was elegant: He wanted to simply ask mothers, "Tell us what you experience when taking care of your baby. We want to know what you do and how you feel about everything that occurs by writing a daily diary. For this we will pay you $5 per day." (Big money in 1961.) After four weeks we collected the dairies. The conclusion was obvious: *The cloth diaper system didn't work.*

Leo put it neatly: "Forget about cost. Design something that works."

I went back to Neenah with the agreement that each time I came up with a new design I would make four and send two to Leo, since we both had kids in diapers.

The old saying is: How do you make a diamond? Heat and pressure. My wife, Madeline, supplied the heat and Leo supplied the pressure.

The criteria for a successful diaper are: soft and absorbent, followed by doesn't leak. Fit and configuration are very important to prevent leaks. The two most obvious components were an outer polyethylene cover (pants) and an inner absorbent layer (diaper), for which we used a fluff web from the maternity pad line. This bat of fluff was wrapped with a 2-ply wrapper of tissue that had excellent capillary action properties.

It didn't take long to find the right baby-side cover because one of Wilson's group had developed a bonded web. This was essentially a Dacron fiber that did not shrink when heated. Though the Dacron was hydrophilic, because of its thinness and the high capillary action of the fluff wrapper, urine was quickly drawn into the absorbent fluff.

The pin replacement came to me when a 3M salesman called on us to drum up new business. We had him sign a confidentiality agreement and I asked him if his tape would work on polyethylene and was it hypo-allergenic, since it would come in contact with a baby?

He realized it was for a diaper and left us some samples of a blue tape. We put on release strips that were similar to those on Band-aids and we had our pins. (I found out many years later that the 3M salesman took credit for the idea of putting tapes on disposable diapers.)

About this time we got hold of some diapers that Procter & Gamble was testing in Peoria. They had a longitudinal fold which would be machine-friendly but bunched up in the crotch.

I spent a day at my desk folding paper. It paid off when I came up with a triangular fold that had the added aesthetic advantage that it *looked* like a diaper.

We made up enough for several days for both Leo's baby and mine.

The next day was a Friday and I spent the evening out with the boys playing cards. I was a bit hung over when Madeline woke me on Saturday morning to tell me Leo was on the phone. He said his boy had slept through the night and had awakened in a dry bed with a full diaper. (Madeline had told me the same thing about our boy.)

Leo said the next step was to make 100 and I told him it would take a few days, since they were all made by hand and hard to fold.

I had spent my summer after high school as a laborer in a carton plant and remembered how cardboard was creased to make it easy to fold. Since we had the equipment to make folding carton dies in the Operational Creativity shop, I went over and made a creasing die and mounted it in a large press that we used for cutting out foam cups and cartons. After a diaper had been creased with the die, the fold just fell into place. An unexpected benefit was that the condensed creases were very fine capillaries and acted as super-wicks to move the moisture throughout the diaper. In a few days we had 100 and I took them down to Chicago.

When Leo described how he planned to use them I

was aghast. He had taken the names of 50 new mothers out of the *Chicago Tribune*. He said the plan was to knock on their doors and tell them we had something for their babies and then tell them we would like to see them use it.

I was quick to correct him and say we would tell them it was a diaper and give them an instruction sheet. Leo then explained how to develop products: "You keep putting up increasingly higher hurdles. When your product doesn't get over them you know what to improve. When you can't think of any higher hurdles, you have a product. I believe this is the last development hurdle. Don't you want to give it the acid test?"

What else could I say but yes? The test was run, two diapers to each mother. Fifty of fifty mothers recognized the product was a diaper; 49 used it correctly the first try.

"We know we have a diaper," said Leo. "Now we have to find out how to talk about it."

He went back to the diary approach and got panels going with different up-front descriptions. Some were told nothing; some were told the product was form-fitting, soft, absorbent, stay-dry liner, tape fasteners, hypo-allergenic, etc.; and some were told a combination of product promises. The result: the more you told the customer. the more likely they were to complain. The less you told them, the more likely they were to be satisfied.

Leo then ran a price test. The panel members were

told the use test was over but we had some samples left that we were willing to sell for 25 cents each. A number of women bought at that price. The rest were told that there was another batch available at 20 cents each and some bought at that price. By the time the offer got to 10 cents, everyone had bought except the few who would not buy at any price.

Leo prognosticated that the problem with this product would be to keep it on the shelf. "Say you get two, maybe three shelf facings. That will hold enough packages to satisfy eight to 12 customers, providing no one buys more than one package. You will be constantly out of stock."

We ran a distribution test in Grand Rapids, Michigan, and it proved Leo right. We could not keep it on the shelf. Go into a modern supermarket and look at the size of the diaper section. Leo was prescient.

All this was lost on the Kimberly-Clark marketing types. They considered the test a failure. Leo was regarded as a charlatan and huckster. Leo didn't help the feeling much as he quickly realized he was talking to empty suits.

Because of my penchant for vulgar candor and complete lack of tact, I was kept in the background as much as possible. Then Jack Kimberly made his statement that working on diapers was like sitting on the bridge and dropping hundred dollar bills into the river.

HOW WE KEPT THE DIAPER ALIVE.

One day, Bill Kimberly, Jack's second son, came by and told us that a friend of his, Dr. Frank Faulkner, the head pediatrician at the University of Louisville hospital, was interested in our diaper. They were constantly having outbreaks of diaper rash and were convinced the culprit was the cloth diaper system We made a modified infant version of the diaper and it dramatically reduced the incidence of diaper rash and umbilicus.

When Bill went over to run the Commercial Department, one of the first things he did was to make newborn diapers. After Procter & Gamble rolled out Pampers, K-C's marketers suddenly realized that the diaper market was real and quickly confiscated Wilson's machine.

Without it they would have been two years behind.

BILL WILSON: THE BUSINESS LIFE-CYCLE.

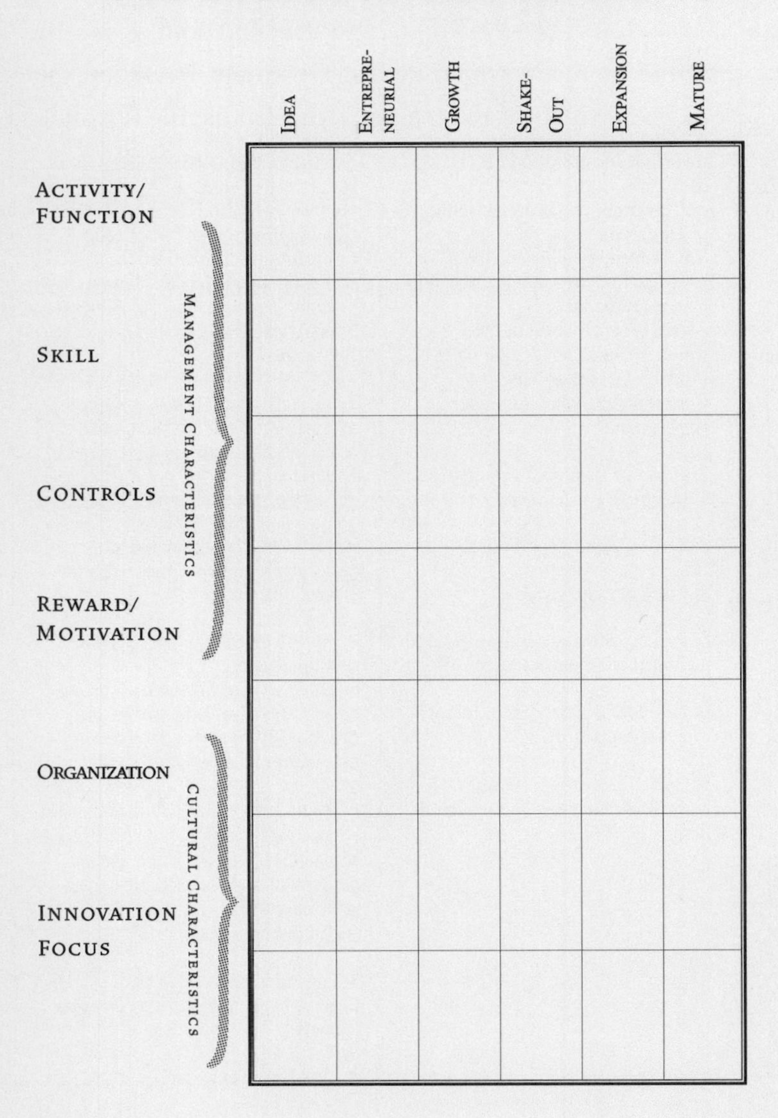

1. IDEA STAGE

MANAGEMENT CHARACTERISTICS

PRIORITIES:

ACTIVITY	SKILL
1: Define opportunities. Investigate—stir things up. Scanning, sifting, sorting, connecting, creating, exploring, pushing, pulling, reflecting. Sift "information" from "data." Evaluate forecasts and social, political, economic trends. Aware of what world desires, wants, needs. Know/ learn what is satisfying this need now. Conceptualize what might be. Experiment. 2: Generate concepts/ prototypes. Touch, feel, try, fix, do. 3: Test different hypothesies. 4: Enter market, validate. 5: Initially integrate consumer need; technical solution and talent. 6: Develop product design for customer acceptability. 7: Capitalize on opportunities. High level of simultaneity and recursiveness.	1: Insatiable learners; curious; open-minded; seeking new experiences. Naturally self-starting. High energy level. Naturally supportive (or trained.) Courageous; self-confident. Self-disciplined. Sense of humor. Tolerant. Positive, creative, innovative outlook. Aware of physical world; sensual; esthetic. 2: Strongly action-oriented; sponsor best cause, even if it is not popular. Knowledgeable about problems and opportunities. Persistent; tenacious; able to keep going when things go wrong. Analytical; able to find direction; turning negatives into positive; using them v. fighting them. 3: Able to listen to others and offer encouragement. Users of disparate resources; able to coordinate multiple resources and activities. Love and passion for product. Embrace ambiguity. 4: Right-brain creative thinkers; make connections readily; synthesize. Good planners; able to see future and its requirements. Able to stimulate and motivate others. 'Legitimate crazies.' 5: Few middle-of-the-roaders. Leaders by example, not by dictating "how to."

Develop a continuous succession of new products based on either technological innovation, strategic innovation, or both.

CONTROL	MOTIVATION
1: Flexibility to control budgets (provide for salaries, expenses, exploratory contracts). Only those controls that stimulate more activity. Overall budget in job-area. No detailed breakdowns. 2: Controlled to a limited number of milestones. Deadlines. 3: Flexibility to manage people. Reviews frequent but irregular and informal. Feed possible projects to death (Reality Test). Feedback on how activity is or isn't meeting organization's objectives	1: Can play the game again; access to money, etc. High sense of freedom. Access to information, people, power, consultants. Self-realization; clear accomplishment; personal development. Stake in outcome. 2: Tightly-held objectives; loose methods. Exhilarating use of whole brain. Contagious enthusiasm. Team spirit; 'The elite.' Self-sufficiency.

MULTIPLE ROLES IN THE IDEA STAGE

CHAMPION: Person who is devoted to a concept and pursues it against all odds. FACILITATOR: Assists the innovation process without taking a judgmental stance. GATEKEEPER: Gathers information from inside, outside company; organizes and reports to appropriate people in timely manner. IDEATOR: Person who likes to generate ideas for their own sake.	INVENTOR: Individual who discovers a phenomenon and then transforms it into a tangible product. ORIGINATOR: Person responsible for the conception and documentation of an idea. SPONSOR: Has the ability to support concepts—especially those likely to be unpopular. Supports development of an idea, forages for resources, provides support, encouragement and cover.

IDEA STAGE

CULTURAL CHARACTERISTICS

PRIORITIES: ↓

ORGANIZATION	ENVIRONMENT
1: Close-knit; small; intimate. Multi-discipline. Informal. Cross-functional skills. 2: Formed around one or more highly-visible individuals. Sensitive management; champion sponsored. Technical skunk works. Search-and-destroy marketing groups. Low differentiation in roles; group establishes norms. 3: Horizontal structure. Dispersed accountability; self-accountability. Technical-licensing search. 4: No "outside department" responsibilities. Full commitment to group.	1: Sheltered; nurturing; family micro-culture. Improvisation; informality. Shared goal: no internal competition. Many experiments going on simultaneously; test and feedback from market. Flexible/ free license to circumvent regular channels, policies, practices. Quick authorization with no certain pay-off. 2: High level of problem-solving and problem-spotting. Sense of purpose. Fast-moving. Failures normal. 3: Adequate time for research and information-gathering. Much individual cross-fertilization. 4: Frequent joint consultation; joint problem-solving.

INNOVATIVE FOCUS	ALERT THINKING
1: Basic product innovation.	1: Seeing connections; ability to put together two or more things that have never been put together before.

CHARACTERISTICS OF THE WORKING ENVIRONMENT

ENVIRONMENT IS BIASED TOWARD LEARNING.
High tolerance for "ambiguity" and "productive" mistakes. Much low-cost ad hoc experimentation. Exploration, especially to find roadblocks (then you know where to work). Use of, but not capitulation to, theory (questioning of conventional theory).

ORGANIZATIONAL FLEXIBILITY.
Horizontal rather than vertical "reporting" relationships. Peer, more than subordinate/ superior management. Ad hoc small groups to invent and solve problems. Most roles shared (everyone does everything). Integrate consumer need, technical solution, talent.

INCLUSIVITY.
Everyone is an expert and has something to offer/ learn. Every concept or fact may have significance. Investigate, collect, scan, sift, sort, explore, comment, create and name. Categorize vs. dispose. Ambiguity, unstructured environment; contained disorder. Playfulness.

SYMBIOSIS.
If you are not both getting and giving intrinsically, then you will have a hard time in this environment. True for both people and concepts/ things. Bias against waste.

WORKING WITH VS. DOMINATING.
Strong bias toward learning the rules of a system (human or technical). Using little (strategically-placed) or no interventions to make things happen (jujitsu the momentum already there), vs. attempting to control the systems.

2. ENTREPRENEURIAL STAGE

MANAGEMENT CHARACTERISTICS

PRIORITIES:

ACTIVITY	SKILL
1: Develop consumer-use tests. Design prototype machines. Refine product design. Specific sales and distribution channels. Take concept and make verification of it real. Get it off the ground. Convince others to allocate resources. 2: Develop budgets. Develop advertising and promotion. Run test-markets; establish targets. 3: Begin manufacturing. Get to market. 4: Require high growth for full-scale production, financial viability. Margin improvements via volume called for more than production-cost savings. Command respect and support from all business functions. 1-4: Do a lot of networking. Define market.	1: Single-minded. Foster trust among diverse parties. Champions and risk-takers. Managers—intuitive business judgment. Marketing experience. Market research knowledge. Product designers. First-of-a-kind machine designers. Respond quickly to setbacks. Create confidence in his/ her vision. Minimize threat to others. Get others to work on the side; coordinator, communicator. Knowledgeable about things and people; resources and uses. Enthusiastic. 2: Practical; strategy implementers. Experience a disadvantage. Follow no-nonsense approach. Deal makers: realize multi-dimensional complexity of top management problems and solutions. Hold opposing truths simultaneously. Rapidly change focus. Identify emergency problems and implement solution in uncharted territory. Sustain effort. Wheeler-dealers. 3: Able to manage competing individuals. Ruthless. Opportunist. Fire/ inspire others.

Gain diversification by establishing a new business based on products fulfilling a basic need in an innovative manner.

CONTROL	MOTIVATION
1: Flexibility to control budgets (provide for salaries, expenses, exploratory contracts). Only those controls that stimulate more activity. Overall budget in job-area. No detailed breakdowns.	1: Set own goals. Able to break rules. Access to resources. High incentives based on fairly nonquantifiable results.
2: Controlled to a limited number of milestones. Deadlines.	2: Performance related. High financial rewards, visibility. Personal growth. External, internal mobility.
3: Flexibility to manage people. Reviews frequent but irregular and informal. Feed possible projects to death (Reality Test). Feedback on how activity is or isn't meeting organization's objectives	3: Low status/ security rewards. New assignments with greater responsibility. Fear of losing face.

COMPARISON OF CHARACTERISTICS

IDEA STAGE	ENTREPRENEUR STAGE
AMBIGUITY: Everything, everyone of potential significance.	PURPOSE/ VISION: Champions foster a vision of the purpose.
EXPLORATION: "Never take no for an answer."	PERSISTENCE: "Never take no for an answer."
NETWORKS: Make explorations new, thorough.	USING NETWORKS: Make explorations new, thorough.
MULTIPLE ROLES: Each person wears several hats.	ROLES DEFINED: Rank not as important as accomplishing task.
GUERRILLA WARFARE AGAINST CONVENTIONAL WISDOM: "The maverick's secret society."	GUERRILLA WARFARE IN THE MARKETPLACE: "Make a little, sell a little."

ENTREPRENEURIAL STAGE

CULTURAL CHARACTERISTICS

PRIORITIES:

ORGANIZATION	ENVIRONMENT
1: Single strong leader. Marketing orientation. Champion who structures own organization with trusted lieutenants. Venture-team with all key skills included. Goal or project-oriented leadership. Mentor and/ or consulting assistance readily available. 2: Few meetings with more than two or three present. Champion is accountable. Cross-functional skills report through product lines, not functional lines. Informal networks. Articulated procedures. Quick. 3: Everyone knows one another. Variety; some differentiation of skills. Multidisciplines represented: manufacturing, marketing and engineering involved from the start. Maintain continuity; permit new members to join. Full support of top management.	1: Driven hard from within. Shared goals; sense of urgency; excitement. Challenging atmosphere; winning spirit. Need for flexible decisiveness. Continuing problem-solving posture. 2: Sense of purpose; dedication to project. Constantly in-touch with consumers; close attention to manufacturing and product. Continuing search for the real market; willingness to change to reach it. 3: Technical and manufacturing areas need to keep improvising, inventing better ways to produce the product. Marketing/ sales improvise/ invent more effective ways to get product to consumers.

INNOVATIVE FOCUS	ALERT THINKING
1: Basic product innovation.	1: Quick reaction to the unexpected. Taking advantage of the unexpected.

CHARACTERISTICS OF THE WORKING ENVIRONMENT

VISION THAT ELECTRIFIES.

The "how" isn't as important as the "what."
People are driven to be first or near-first to market or to develop the new/ better product/ process.
The team as leader.

'DOING,' MORE THAN PLANNING.

Bias toward getting things done with sense of urgency.
Little regard for procedures and rules.
Shared rewards.
Team has a stake in the outcome, whether financial, other-than-financial, or both.

INFORMALITY.

While there is a central leader and team members have specific responsibilities, their loyalty is to the team and getting things done more than to their role and its duties.
Requires comfort with role-ambiguity.

NETWORKING.

Using a network of both human and other-than-human resources when needed.

3. GROWTH STAGE

MANAGEMENT CHARACTERISTICS

PRIORITIES:

ACTIVITY	SKILL
1: Create and change the organization. Penetrate market. Establish good growth to consolidate entry. Watch market like a hawk.	1: Plan for success. Strong interpersonal skills. Astute marketing orientation. Able to set priorities. Decisive, demanding. Fire others but remain above.
2: Complete product line. Establish national sales and distribution.	2: Create urgency. Extremely demanding of selves and others; workaholic. Excellent hiring, training, expansion-planning, and execution abilities.
3: Attention to market segmentation and product spin-off. Wear many hats at once. Investigate production improvements. Organize improvements and consolidate. Experience heaviest cash-flow drain.	3: Traditional business-development experience; vision for new business and its ramifications. Not afraid to make mistakes. Politically savvy. High integrity. Strategy implementers. Follow entrepreneurial tactics. Good administrators, but show flexibility.
4: Generate considerable PR. Plan for next stage.	

Increase market penetration. Improve profitability by rapid exploitation of successful entrepreneurial ventures.

CONTROL	MOTIVATION
1: Sales, distribution share targets. Budget in smaller units. Formal review system. Expense budget (losses on sales). 2: Market share, sales and distribution critical. 3: Viewed as non-punishing so as not to stunt growth; off-site meetings to check progress. Periodic review of results by related business functions. Human resources: numbers, recruitment and allocation closely managed. Inventory very important. 4: Long product-development cycles. Decisions made by central staffs on technical issues.	1: Authority to make decisions. High-performance base—as high as possible within overall system. High incentives with more quantitative measures. High risk/ high reward. Considerable amount of time and anxiety expended. Opportunity for long-term significant payback clear. 2: Promotion. Achievement. 3: Stability: "We made it!" 4: Financial rewards taper off.

GROWTH STAGE

CULTURAL CHARACTERISTICS

PRIORITIES: ↓

ORGANIZATION	ENVIRONMENT
1: Clear procedures. Rapid, flexible communication; quick responses. Frequent charges. Cross-functional groups frequently created and discarded. Overall business organization begins to form. Department organizations with sales and R&D included. 2: Large teams integrated. Often driven by where individuals are, not company needs. Regular small meetings; well-developed plans. Operations orientation. Functional centralization; promote good sharing of learnings and economies of scale. 3: Product differentiation. Formal. Administrative support added. More functional accountability to promote teamwork. 4: Vertical structure.	1: Network of relationships in both product and sales. Positive, friendly environment. Ability to recognize and promote people with managerial capabilities. 2: Improvises/ invents ways to achieve and maintain closeness between R&D, manufacturing, marketing and sales. Innovates/ invents product improvements, line extensions, manufacturing efficiencies, new products to join the family. 3: Understands and models to achieve and maintain relationships as people multiply. Prepares for and practices cost-cutting to deal with new competition.

INNOVATIVE FOCUS	ALERT THINKING
1: Product-improvement innovation. 2: Recycled from basic process innovation (product improvement innovation).	1: Recognizing time to change organization. 2: Recognizing when to establish centralized and decentralized controls.

DEFINITIONS OF INNOVATIONS.

TECHNOLOGICAL INNOVATION:

An innovation driven by new proprietary technical insight based on engineering, scientific principles, and research.

STRATEGIC INNOVATION:

An innovation based on new strategic insights gained from observation of the world at large and the basic social, political, economic, ecological, environmental, scientific and market trends.
Business-oriented, based on developing a competitive advantage by changing the rules of the game or creating a new game.
Satisfying the new in a better way.

4. Consolidation/ Shake-Out Stage

Management Characteristics

Priorities: (arrow pointing down, 1 to 4)

Activity	Skill
1: Constantly appraises portfolio. Reassesss organizational goals. Manage paradoxically. 2: Gain market-share. Add line extensions. Reduce product cost. Improve product. Focus on cost-cutting, investments.	1: Have deep pockets and convictions—good strategic survival plan. Find right people. Deal with multiple perspectives. Self-confident; ambitious. Astute planners. Simplify, concentrate—not easily distracted. Vision and foresight for developing a range of options. Good information flow. 2: Analytical. Logical. Cool-headed; reliable. Mental toughness. Quickly makes decisions. Leaders inspire loyalty. 3: Willing to consider new approaches. Change easily. Fighters. Create belief and trust. 4: Good poker players. Negotiators. Convey justice.
Control	**Motivation**
1: Head-count. Visible and efficient reporting. Market-awareness. 2: Flexibility in managing people. Market share. Product preference over competition. Product quality. ROA objective. 3: Product analyses added. 4: Presently and five years in future. Formal authority systems and procedures.	1: Profit-related rewards. Golden handcuffs. 2: Visible authority. Challenge; responsibility. Personal and departmental survival. 3: Rivalry.

If business is a good one—large, profitable—it attracts many competitors. Prices fall. Value for money needed. Shake-out occurs.

CULTURAL CHARACTERISTICS

ORGANIZATION	ENVIRONMENT
1: Simplified from growth. Task forces. Frequent small meetings. Strong upward communication. Flexibility at top. General vision communicated. 2: Financial/ administrative orientation. Functional differentiation. Support of top management important. 3: Heavy emphasis on international growth. Outsiders employed at higher levels. Inside individuals less committed to project, have only a piece of responsibility.	1: Driven hard from outside. Formalized organizational structure. Active, constantly-changing environment. 2: Development of systems, controls, reviews. Four separate constituencies identified: customers, communities, employees, society at large. 3: Innovate/ invent new ways to market, sell, distribute product. Innovate/ invent continuous small improvements and line-extensions. Technical and manufacturing areas keep innovating and inventing better ways to produce the product.
INNOVATIVE FOCUS	**ALERT THINKING**
1: Product-improvement innovation. Process-improvement innovation. 2: Marketing, distribution, selling, advertising, promotion innovations.	1: Continual consciousness of competition (strategy, tactics, cost, product value). 2: Quick reaction to marketplace changes. 3: Constant contact with end-user's perceptions. 4: Advantage taken of any unexpected opening.

5. EXPANSION STAGE

MANAGEMENT CHARACTERISTICS

PRIORITIES: (ordered from top to bottom)

ACTIVITY	SKILL
1: Weed-out loser products. Consolidate investments. Recognize importance of competitive stance. Protect the "cash cow." Plan and cull. 2: Maintain low but positive growth. Annually improve key products and properties. Reduce product costs. Disburse resources. 3: Reinvest on small scale. Add select extensions (related products). Save.	1: Sense of direction: structured; good judgment. Social skills: adept in human relations for sales, service, distributors, retailers. Persuasive: influences people. Experienced in marketing, business. Self-confident; decisive. 2: Analytical thinker. Deliberate, cautious, able to think in depth. Understand limits but willing to take risks. Always seeking improvements. Adaptable; flexible. 3: Understand legal and governmental restraints. Able to say no; tough. Good planners. Traditional marketing background. Product improvement-oriented. Cost reducers. Cautiously extend market.
CONTROLS	**MOTIVATION**
1: All aspects of plan set by management. Control of product, sales, cost and expense budgets. Control of growth plan. 2: Formal authority. Rulebooks. ROA and cash-flow targets. Product preference. Quality.	1: Status-oriented awards, especially for ingenuity. Honor and symbols, Promotion, title. 2: Dollar-base salary and performance bonus. High perquisites. Successful team.

Extend the business; build on opportunities.

Cultural Characteristics

Organization	Environment
1: Large business department. Large R&D staff. Matrix management. Steady routines. 2: Geographical and functional. Outsiders at middle levels. Large meetings. Dual organizations: marketing, operations parallel. Department differentiation and opportunities for cross-communication.	1: Generally predictable world in which to operate. 2: Careful; cautious; conservative. 3: Plans and planning have prime importance. Emerging superior product—sets standard for industry. Markets coalesce. Performance, reliability, sales, service become important. 4: Organization: line and staff grows large. 5: Numerous market-research studies necessary. 6: Continual product/ process improvements. Experimental within but external rivalry.
Innovative focus	**Alert Thinking**
1: Process-improvement; incremental product improvement. Promotion innovation becomes important. 2: Strive for basic product innovation. Need for innovation in work practices.	1: Careful analysis of all information. 2: Deliberate, cautious, conservative judgment.

6. Mature Stage

Management Characteristics

Priorities: (top to bottom)

Activity	Skill
1: Maximize bottom-line gracefully. Reassess assets. Maximizing cash integral with stagnant or declining share. Reduce overhead costs; consolidate. 2: Low investment, if at all. 3: Focus on efficiency of work practices. Make transition to death or renewal.	1: "Squeezing the turnip." Accurate, analytical; attention to detail. Interested in figures and analysis. Cautious, reliable, deliberate. Retrenchers: cut excess staff, costs, services. Dependable; good negotiators. 2: Make tough human resources choices. Good judgment in forecasting, estimating future. Fine administrators; high delegation; lets go. Adaptable; good judgment and business sense. Adroit at shaking-up. 3: Customer- and service-oriented.
Controls	**Motivation**
1: Cost-reduction program. 2: Maintains share or sells share for maximum price. Analyzes deviations from standard. Invests minimum.	1: High base salary. 2: Predictable career-path. 3: Security rewards and bonus. Power symbols. Honor. 4: Process orientation, e.g. "A Job Well Done."

Harvest the present business; manage for cash.

CULTURAL CHARACTERISTICS

ORGANIZATION	ENVIRONMENT
1: Traditional. Spartan. Run lean on staff. 2: Memos more important than meetings.	1: Deliberate, predictable outside world. 2: Tightly-controlled inside world. 3: Ultimate in systems, procedures, check-offs, etc. 4: Standardized manufacturing, distribution, selling and product design. Efficient: volume very important. 5: Entire industry becomes rigid. Takes minimal risks. Little innovation.
INNOVATIVE FOCUS	**ALERT THINKING**
1: Work practices. 2: Basic product innovation.	1: Sharp, accurate analysis of present and future. 2: Inspired conceptualizing of future.

BUSINESS LIFE-CYCLE: SYSTEM CHARACTERISTICS

	HIGH PERFORMANCE (BREAKTHROUGH)	MAINTENANCE (COPING)	SELF-DESTRUCTIVE
LEADERSHIP/ PURPOSE	High sense of shared purpose.	Widely disparate or uncommitted.	Little or no sense of purpose.
LEADERSHIP BEHAVIOR	Skills and understanding of managerial process highly prized and developed.	Widely disparate or uncommitted.	Negative or neglected.
MODELING BEHAVIOR	Leader and others visibly model behavior they expect of others.	Leaders frequently pay little attention to impact of own behavior.	Usually model negative norms.
LEVEL OF BELIEF	High belief in possibilities in others and in self.	Limited belief in possibilities	Little or no belief in self or in others.
CONCERN FOR HEALTH	High concern for positive wellness aspects of personal health.	Concern for not being sick.	Little concern for health—many negative health practices.
VALUE & TASK OF PEOPLE	Value both in maximum degree.	Emphasize task over people	Value neither.
VALUING PEOPLE	Honors and values any person.	Honors and values some.	No one.
TRUST & OPENNESS	High level.	Limited.	High distrust; "closed-off" communication.
INDEPENDENCE; INTERDEPENDENCE	Recognize need people have for one another as a virtue and celebrates it.	Inter- and intradependence in conflict; sometimes chooses one over the other.	Consider important that everyone do everything on his/her own.

HIGH PERFORMANCE (BREAKTHROUGH)	MAINTENANCE (COPING)	SELF-DESTRUCTIVE	
Flexible, clear, open.	Traditional.	Rigid.	ROLE DEFINITION
Emphasis on involving people in decisions affecting them.	Involve only when necessary, usually in routine ways.	Seldom involve others in decisions affecting them.	DECISION-MAKING
Highly valued; major attention to the process of innovating.	Largely routine; little attention.	Usually model negative norms.	CREATIVITY
Prudent and creative.	Limited—largely routine.	No risk taken that is not *essential.*	RISK-TAKING
Everyone assumes responsibility.	A few assume responsibility, then drive others.	People avoid responsibility.	ASSUMING RESPONSIBILITY
Simultaneous, with maximum emphasis on both individual and culture.	Tend to focus on individuals only.	Little concern for either.	CONCERN WITH ORGANIZATION'S CULTURE
Expect success; view problems as opportunities to learn, improve.	Focus on identifying problems and coping.	Expect failure.	SUCCESS ORIENTATION
Usually seen as a joy and a pleasure.	Way of earning a living.	A problem—to be avoided whenever possible.	WORK ORIENTATION
Pro-active in relation to problems and opportunities.	Re-active and coping.	Slow to react—allow problems to become chronic.	PRO-ACTIVE, REACTIVE ORIENTATION

	HIGH PERFORMANCE (BREAKTHROUGH)	MAINTENANCE (COPING)	SELF-DESTRUCTIVE
CONFLICT RESOLUTION	All win.	Win/ Lose.	All lose.
CHANGE STRATEGIES	Use systematic, culture-based long-range change strategies.	Piecemeal short-term strategies.	Not concerned with, victimized by change.
PLANNING	Seen as creative, useful process.	Routine, bureaucratic.	Little—mostly firefighting.
SYNERGY	Positive, exponential.	None: additive only.	Negative—exponential.
COMPANY EXPECTATIONS	Expect company's activities to make an enormous difference.	Expect to make little or no difference.	Expect to make a negative difference.

The Maverick Network

Books are permanent—and therein lies a problem. The Maverick Way is, if nothing else, a rapidly-mutating area of excitement and inquiry, conjecture and (even) contention.

What's a maverick or MOM (or even a maverick-protector) to do?

Three Web sites have been created to serve as way points, resources, and even refuges for mavericks. They are kept up-to-date by people who understand computers and this stuff called "html."

Innovationsthatwork.com is hosted by Vincent & Associates, and focuses on Lanny's practice in the areas of strategic invention, market discovery, and entrepreneurial planning.

Hot-button out of that site into the **Maverick Network**, a group of people who are pondering and pursuing the Maverick Way. The site has profiles of network members, e-mail addresses for instant networking, and the latest updates on plans for the annual Mavericks Roundtable.

Maverickway.com focuses on the book you are now holding. It offers excerpts, Louis Dunn illustrations, and ample opportunities to purchase more books. Visit often.

Resource Index

How is the maverick managed?

What are the Maverick's characteristics?